YOUR
Best Life
BEGINS EACH
MORNING

YOUR
Best Life
BEGINS EACH MORNING

Devotions to Start Every
New Day of the Year

JOEL OSTEEN

Faith
Words

NEW YORK • BOSTON • NASHVILLE

Unless otherwise indicated, Scriptures are taken from the HOLY BIBLE: NEW INTERNATIONAL VERSION®. Copyright © 1973, 1978, 1984 by International Bible Society. Used by permission of Zondervan Publishing House. All rights reserved.

Scriptures noted AMP are taken from the Amplified® Bible. Copyright © 1954, 1962, 1965, 1987 by The Lockman Foundation. Used by permission.

Scriptures noted NASB are taken from the New American Standard Bible®, Copyright © 1960, 1962, 1963, 1968, 1972, 1975, 1977, 1995 by The Lockman Foundation. Used by permission.

Scriptures noted NKJV are taken from the NEW KING JAMES VERSION. Copyright © 1979, 1980, 1982, Thomas Nelson, Inc., Publishers.

Scriptures noted TLB are taken from *The Living Bible,* copyright © 1971. Used by permission of Tyndale House Publishers, Inc., Wheaton, Illinois 60189. All rights reserved.

Scriptures noted NLT are taken from the *Holy Bible,* New Living Translation, copyright © 1996. Used by permission of Tyndale House Publishers, Inc., Wheaton, Illinois 60189. All rights reserved.

Scriptures noted The Message are from The Message. Copyright © 1993, 1994, 1995, 1996, 2000, 2001, 2002. Used by permission of NavPress Publishing Group.

Scriptures noted KJV are taken from the King James Version of the Bible.

Literary development and design: Koechel Peterson & Associates, Inc., Minneapolis, Minnesota.

Portions of this book have been adapted from *Your Best Life Now,* copyright © 2004 and *Daily Readings from Your Best Life Now,* copyright © 2005 by Joel Osteen. Published by FaithWords.

FaithWords
Hachette Book Group
237 Park Avenue, New York, NY 10017
Visit our Web site at www.faithwords.com.

The FaithWords name and logo are trademarks of Hachette Book Group.

Printed in Singapore.

First Printing: December 2008

10 9 8 7 6 5 4 3 2
ISBN-10: 0-446-54509-0
ISBN-13: 978-0-446-54509-9

Library of Congress Control Number: 2008931464

My voice shalt thou hear in the morning,
O LORD; in the morning will I direct
my prayer unto thee, and will look up.

PSALM 5:3 KJV

Introduction

THE KEY TO LIVING YOUR best life starts with how you approach every new morning, because today is the only day you have. You can't do anything about the past, and you don't know what the future holds. But when you wake up in the morning, you can make up your mind to do your best to enjoy your day. You're not going to allow what does or doesn't happen to steal your joy and keep you from God's abundant life.

Don't start your day off by feeling guilty about yesterday or recalling all the mistakes you made. Rather, when you make mistakes, simply ask God for forgiveness and then move on, confident that the moment you ask, God forgives you. You are ready for a great present and a bright future.

Get up every morning and receive God's love and mercy and the power of His Word for your life. Start your day with God by saying, "Father, I thank You that this is going to be a great day. I thank You that I have discipline, self-control; that I make good decisions. I may not have done all that I could have yesterday, but that day's gone. I'm going to get up and do better today."

These devotions are written to inspire ardent love and worship to God. While they are not meant to replace your personal time with God, it is my desire that the readings will be keys you can use to unlock doors leading a fuller life. I hope they will be a springboard to help you draw nearer to God and to help you overcome the obstacles that might keep you from living your best life now.

Your life can be transformed and renewed as you allow God's Word to refresh and to reshape your thinking, speaking, and daily activities. Allow the Scriptures to speak to you. Be still and listen to what God is saying to you. No matter where you are or what challenges you face, you can start to enjoy your life right now!

YOUR *Best Life*

BEGINS EACH MORNING

*For I am about to do something new.
See, I have already begun! Do you
not see it? I will make a pathway
through the wilderness. I will create
rivers in the dry wasteland.*

ISAIAH 43:19 NLT

Unpack Your *Dreams*

WHAT DO YOU WANT TO DO with your life? If you could write your best life story this morning, what would it say? Is your first reaction to see and describe yourself in terms of past experiences or present limitations, more in terms of losing or just surviving rather than fulfilling your dreams?

If you've packed away your dreams, dare to unpack them today and ask God to rekindle them in your heart and mind. It's time to *enlarge your vision*. He wants to pour out His far and beyond favor on you (see Ephesians 2:7). He wants to do big things and new things in your life.

We Serve a *Great* God

"For I know the plans I have for you," declares the LORD, *"plans to prosper you and not to harm you, plans to give you hope and a future."*
JEREMIAH 29:11

YOU MAY HAVE EXPERIENCED adversity or trials in your past. Perhaps you've had more than your share of setbacks and heartaches. But today is a brand-new day. It is time to stretch your faith and pursue the excellence that God has placed in your heart. It is time to break out of the "barely get by" mentality, to become the best you can be, not merely average or ordinary, for the rest of your life.

We serve the Most High God, and His dream for your life is so much bigger and better than you can even imagine. Never settle for a small view of God. Start thinking as God thinks. Think big. Think increase. Think abundance. Think more than enough!

What, then, shall we say in response to this? If God is for us, who can be against us? He who did not spare his own Son, but gave him up for us all— how will he not also, along with him, graciously give us all things?

ROMANS 8:31–32

With God on *Your* Side

GOD IS CONSTANTLY trying to plant new seeds in your heart. He's trying to fill you with so much hope and expectancy that the seed will grow and bring forth a tremendous harvest.

Never allow negative thinking to keep you from God's best. If you will get in agreement with God, this can be the greatest time of your life. With God on your side, you cannot possibly lose. He can make a way when it looks as though there is none. He can open doors that no one can shut. He can cause you to be at the right place, at the right time. He can supernaturally turn your dreams into reality.

Stretch *Your* Faith

For therein is the righteousness of God revealed from faith to faith: as it is written, The just shall live by faith.

ROMANS 1:17 KJV

ERHAPS WE HAVE A GOAL to break a bad habit, to lose some weight, or to pay off our credit cards. At first, we're so excited and we go after it! But over time, we get lazy; we get complacent. Maybe we see a little improvement, but then we get comfortable right where we are. *Where we are* may not be a bad place, but we know it's not where we're supposed to be. We're not stretching our faith. We're not pursuing the excellence that God has placed in our hearts.

Maybe you've been coasting lately, thinking that perhaps you've reached your limits. You're not stretching your faith. You aren't believing for an increase. No, don't stop halfway; go on up to the top of your mountain. Believe God for more.

By faith Abraham, when called to go to a place he would later receive as his inheritance, obeyed and went, even though he did not know where he was going.

HEBREWS 11:8

Step Out of Your *Comfort* Zone

PEOPLE WHO SEE THEIR DREAMS come to pass are people who have some resolve, some backbone; people who refuse to settle for somewhere along the way. Abraham, one of the Old Testament heroes of faith, obeyed God and followed Him all the way to the Promised Land of abundance in Canaan. Abraham's father, however, stopped along the way and settled in Haran (see Genesis 11:31), feeling it was good enough but missing out on God's best.

Don't fall into a complacency trap. It doesn't take any more effort to stay filled with faith than it takes to develop a negative attitude. Dare to step out of your comfort zone today. God has so much more in store. Keep pursuing and keep believing.

Don't Stop Now

Terah took his son Abram, ...
and together they set out from Ur
of the Chaldeans to go to Canaan.
But when they came to Haran,
they settled there.

GENESIS 11:31

WHY DID TERAH STOP THERE? No doubt it was difficult traveling with his flocks, herds, family members, and all of their possessions four thousand years ago. Finally, Terah said, "I can't go any farther. I know this isn't the Promised Land, but let's just settle here; it's good enough."

Maybe like Abraham's father you've already settled halfway, and you've gotten comfortable where you are. I'm challenging you to pull up your stakes, pack your tents, get your belongings, and start moving forward. You are made for more than good enough. Enlarge your vision! You may have had a delay, but that's okay; you can begin again this very morning.

*Be strong and take heart, all you
who hope in the LORD.*

PSALM 31:24

Expand Your Horizons

*P*ERHAPS WE STARTED WITH big dreams in our hearts—we're going to excel in our careers, excel as parents, excel in our walks with God. We get started, but then things get difficult, and achieving our goals doesn't happen as quickly as we had hoped. Discouragement sets in, and we start to give up.

Look yourself in the mirror and say, "I am not going to settle for mediocrity. Nothing may be going my way right now, but I'm going to trust God to help me expand my horizons and keep believing for all that He has for me. I'm going to make it." Focus on your goal, set your course, and have the attitude, *I'm going to reach my full potential in God. I'm going to start living my best life now!*

Get a *New* Vision

Do you have eyes but fail to see, and ears but fail to hear? And don't you remember?

MARK 8:18

HOW'S YOUR SPIRITUAL VISION this morning? Are you focusing on your problems, on what you can't do, on what you can't have? The barrier is in your mind. It's not God's lack of resources or your lack of talent that holds you back. It's simply because you are focused on the wrong things.

Your vision of who you are and what you can become has a tremendous impact in your life. You need to start allowing God to use your imagination to build you up, to help you accomplish your dreams. In other words, keep things in front of you that you want to see come to pass. Take out the paintbrush of faith, hope, and expectancy and begin painting a bright future on the canvas of your heart.

The eye is the lamp of the body; so then if your eye is clear, your whole body will be full of light. But if your eye is bad, your whole body will be full of darkness. If then the light that is in you is darkness, how great is the darkness!

MATTHEW 6:22–23 NASB

See Yourself *Rising*

EACH OF US HAS A PICTURE of ourselves in our imaginations. That "self-image" is similar to a thermostat in a room. It sets the standard at which you will function. You will never consistently rise higher than the image you have of yourself, and you will never accomplish things that you don't first see yourself accomplishing.

If you can learn to look at life through your eyes of faith and start seeing yourself rising to new levels—seeing yourself accomplishing your dreams, receiving more, giving more, loving more, and enjoying life, seeing your family serving God—you'll experience God's blessings and favor.

Focus on *Your* Goals

Listen to me, you who pursue righteousness and who seek the LORD: Look to the rock from which you were cut and to the quarry from which you were hewn.

ISAIAH 51:1

WE PRODUCE WHAT WE continually keep in front of us. If you focus on an image of success in your mind, you're going to move toward success, but if you see yourself as barely getting by, your marriage getting worse, your health going downhill, then most likely your life will gravitate toward those negative situations.

Your vision, what you see, has a tremendous impact in your life. We need to quit allowing our imaginations to keep us beaten down. Instead, let's start allowing God to use our imaginations to build us up. In other words, keep the goals you want to see come to pass in front of you. That image will set the limits for your life.

Then the LORD took Abram outside and said to him, "Look up into the sky and count the stars if you can. That's how many descendants you will have!"

GENESIS 15:5 NLT

Eyes of *Faith*

WHY DID GOD TELL ABRAHAM to go out and look at the stars after He promised he was going to be the father of many nations? Because God knew Abraham needed to get a picture of it in his mind. Abraham and Sarah were old and childless, and in the natural, it was an impossible situation. But whenever Abraham looked up at the stars, he was reminded of God's promise. He began to see the promise through eyes of faith.

You can't give birth to a dream you have not first conceived. You must conceive it on the inside through your eyes of faith before it will come to pass on the outside. Change what you're seeing, and you will change what you're producing.

Break the Curse

So Moses made a bronze snake and put it up on a pole. Then when anyone was bitten by a snake and looked at the bronze snake, he lived.

NUMBERS 21:9

DO YOU KNOW YOUR FAITH can function negatively just as easily as it will function positively? For instance, if your family has a long history of sickness and disease, don't sit back and see yourself the same way: "Well, I guess this is my lot in life."

No, you—more than anybody else—need to start developing a new picture. You need to see yourself as strong, healthy, and living a long, satisfied life. You can be the one to break that curse of ill health. But the first thing you must do is change the image you have of yourself on the inside. Get a new vision. Make sure your eyes are filled with light.

When you see the tassels, you will remember and obey all the commands of the Lord instead of following your own desires and defiling yourselves, as you are prone to do.

NUMBERS 15:39 NLT

The Value of Memories

I LIKE TO PUT THINGS IN FRONT of me that remind me of good times in the past, while expanding my vision for better experiences in the future. I suggest you consider putting things up in your home or office that build your faith—perhaps photos that bring back good memories or show you living life to the full. When you look at those pictures, don't just say, "I wish I was still that happy," or, "I wish I could still fit in that size dress."

No, let the image sink deep down inside you. Don't let the good things God has done in your life slip away. To produce it on the outside, you must first picture it on the inside.

Keep *God's* Word Visible

These commandments that I give you today are to be upon your hearts. Impress them on your children. Talk about them when you sit at home and when you walk along the road, when you lie down and when you get up.... Write them on the doorframes of your houses and on your gates.

DEUTERONOMY 6:6–8, 9

TO BUILD YOURSELF UP SPIRITUALLY and keep you filled with faith, you may benefit from decorating your home with Scripture verses. On the bathroom mirror or where you get dressed, place Scriptures such as "I can do all things through Christ" or "This is the day the Lord has made." On the refrigerator, remind yourself, "God always causes me to triumph." At the back door, place the truth "God's favor is surrounding me like a shield" or "Goodness and mercy are following me today." Put up things that help you to have a big vision for your life.

Neither do men pour new wine into old wineskins. If they do, the skins will burst, the wine will run out and the wineskins will be ruined. No, they pour new wine into new wineskins, and both are preserved.

MATTHEW 9:17

Renew Your Attitude

HAVE YOU ASSUMED THAT you've reached your limits in life, that you will never be more successful or do something meaningful or enjoy the good things in life that you've seen others enjoy? Sad to say, you are exactly right…unless you are willing to change your thinking and start believing for something bigger.

Interestingly, when Jesus wanted to encourage His followers to enlarge their visions, He reminded them, "You can't put new wine into old wineskins." He was saying that you cannot have a larger life with restricted attitudes. Today, will you stretch your faith and vision and get rid of those old negative mind-sets that hold you back?

Reach Out by *Faith*

For she said to herself, "If only I may touch His garment, I shall be made well." But Jesus turned around, and when He saw her He said, "Be of good cheer, daughter; your faith has made you well."

MATTHEW 9:21–22 NKJV

ONE FELLOW WHOSE MARRIAGE was on the verge of dissolution told me, "Joel, I've been this way for a long time. Nothing good ever happens to me. I don't see how my marriage can be restored. We've always had these problems."

"Those wrong attitudes will keep you from receiving the good things God wants to pour out in your life," I told him. "Stop dwelling on negative, destructive thoughts that keep you in a rut. Your life will change when you change your thinking." God has so much more in store for him, and for you as well. If you want to see God's far and beyond favor, you have to start believing it, seeing it, and speaking it.

He did this that He might clearly demonstrate through the ages to come the immeasurable (limitless, surpassing) riches of His free grace (His unmerited favor) in [His] kindness and goodness of heart toward us in Christ Jesus.

EPHESIANS 2:7 AMP

Expect God's Blessings

GOD WANTS THIS TO BE THE BEST time of your life. But if you are going to receive this favor, you must enlarge your vision. You can't go around thinking negative, defeated, limiting thoughts. *Well, I've gone as far as my career will allow.* Or, *I've had this problem for so long; I guess it's just a part of me.*

To experience God's immeasurable favor, you must start expecting His blessings. Start thinking bigger. Get rid of any old negative mind-set. If you will make room for increase in your own thinking, God will bring those things to pass. But God will not pour fresh, creative ideas and blessings into old attitudes.

Expect Great Things

Everything is possible for him who believes.

MARK 9:23

WITH GOD, ALL THINGS ARE POSSIBLE. Wrap your faith and heart around this truth this morning. Let the seeds God is placing in your life take root so they can grow. Expect God's favor to help you break out of the ruts and rise to new heights. It can happen without a bank loan or having the right education. It can happen in spite of your past and what the critics are telling you.

You don't have to be bound by the barriers of the past. Start making room in your thinking for what God has in store for you. Expect to excel in whatever you do. Allow that seed to take root. Get beyond the barriers of the past and expect God to do great things in your life.

It shall be done to you according to your faith.

MATTHEW 9:29 NASB

By *God's* Power

THIS IS YOUR TIME FOR INCREASE. You may have been sick for a long time, but this is your time to get well. You may be bound by addictions and bad habits, but this is the time to be set free. You may be struggling financially, but this is the time for promotion. The key is to believe.

God is saying to you something similar to what the angel told the Virgin Mary—that she would conceive without knowing a man. In other words, God was saying it would happen through supernatural means. What He wants to do in your life is not going to be by your might or power. It's going to be by His Spirit. The power of the Most High God shall come upon you and cause it to happen.

You *Can* Be It

When they had crossed, Elijah said to Elisha, "Tell me, what can I do for you before I am taken from you?" "Let me inherit a double portion of your spirit," Elisha replied. "You have asked a difficult thing," Elijah said, "yet if you see me when I am taken from you, it will be yours—otherwise not."

2 KINGS 2:9–10

HE OLD TESTAMENT PROPHET Elijah experienced numerous miracles, and his understudy, Elisha, witnessed many of them. In their final conversation, Elijah told Elisha, "If God allows you to see it, you can count on your request being granted"; but we can't help but wonder if Elijah was also saying, "If you can see it, you can be it. If you can visualize it, seeing it through the screen of God's Word with your 'spiritual eyes,' it can become a reality in your life."

Remember, low expectations trap you in mediocrity; high expectations motivate and propel you to move forward in life.

Set your minds and keep them set on what is above (the higher things), not on the things that are on the earth.

COLOSSIANS 3:2 AMP

Raise *Your* Level of Expectancy

GOD IS EXTREMELY INTERESTED in what you see through your "spiritual eyes." If you have a vision for victory in your life, you can rise to a new level. But as long as your gaze is on the ground instead of on your possibilities, you risk moving in the wrong direction and missing out on the great things God wants to do in and through you.

It is a spiritual as well as a psychological fact: we move toward what we see in our minds. Your life will follow your *expectations.* What you expect is what you will get. If you raise your level of expectancy, you will enlarge your vision. This could be the day you see your miracle.

The *King* of Kings

No eye has seen, no ear has heard, no mind has conceived what God has prepared for those who love him.

1 CORINTHIANS 2:9

YEARS AGO, A FAMOUS GOLFER accepted an invitation from the king of Saudi Arabia to play golf together for several days. After enjoying their time together, the king asked the golfer what he wanted as a gift—"anything you want." The king insisted that he must be given something, so the golfer finally gave in and said, "Okay, fine. I collect golf clubs. Why don't you give me a golf club?" Weeks went by, and the golfer imagined possibly receiving a solid gold putter or a diamond-studded sand wedge from the oil-rich king until a certified letter arrived. Inside he discovered a deed to a five-hundred-acre golf course in America.

Sometimes kings think differently than you and I think. And friend, we serve the King of kings. Dream accordingly!

Faith is being sure of what we hope for and certain of what we do not see.

HEBREWS 11:1

Good Things Coming

*I*T'S IMPORTANT THAT YOU program your mind for success. If you dwell on positive thoughts, your life will move in that direction; if you continually think negative thoughts, you will live a negative life. If you expect defeat, failure, or mediocrity, your subconscious mind will make sure that you lose, fail, or sabotage every attempt to push above average.

You must think positive thoughts of victory, of abundance, of favor, of hope. Each day, you must choose to live with an attitude that expects good things to happen to you. Start your day with faith and set your mind in the right direction, then go out expecting the favor of God. Expect to excel in your career and rise above life's challenges. Believe God for a great future. You have good things coming!

Break Out of Prison

Why are you downcast, O my soul? Why so disturbed within me? Put your hope in God, for I will yet praise him, my Savior and my God.

PSALM 42:11

ONE OF THE COMMON SLOGANS among men and women who are serving long sentences in federal prison is "You've got nothin' comin'." It's a sad, hopeless statement, robbing the inmates of what little hope they have left. "Nothing is going to change in your life. You're getting what you deserve." Sadly, many people "on the outside" are living behind self-imposed bars, in prisons of their own making, and have succumbed to the same type of thinking. *This is the best you can expect. It isn't going to get any better, so you might as well sit down, keep quiet, and endure it.*

No! You can break out of that prison! The door is unlocked. Start expecting doors of opportunity to open for you, and they will.

Brethren, I do not count myself to have apprehended; but one thing I do, forgetting those things which are behind and reaching forward to those things which are ahead, I press toward the goal for the prize of the upward call of God in Christ Jesus.

PHILIPPIANS 3:13–14 NKJV

Stop Limiting God

WHAT DOES GOD HAVE in store for you today? His dream for your life is so much greater than you can imagine. If God showed you everything He has in store for you, it would boggle your mind.

It's time to quit limiting God. Remember: God is your source, and His creativity and resources are unlimited! God may give you a dream or an idea for an invention, a book, a song, or a movie. One idea from God can forever change the course of your life. God is not limited by what you have or don't have. He can do anything, if you will simply stop limiting Him in your thinking.

Begin Looking *Beyond*

Let us acknowledge the LORD; let us press on to acknowledge him. As surely as the sun rises, he will appear; he will come to us like the winter rains, like the spring rains that water the earth.

HOSEA 6:3

*M*ANY PEOPLE MISS PIVOTAL opportunities in their lives because they've grown accustomed to the status quo. They refuse to make room in their own thinking for the new things God wants to do in their lives. When a great opportunity comes along, rather than launching out in faith, they say, "Well, that could never happen to me. That's just too good to be true."

You may be thinking, *I'll just work at my same job for the rest of my life. This is all I know how to do.* No, God may intervene in your situation and open a better position for you. Today, begin looking beyond where you are to where you want to be.

In that day men will look to their
Maker and turn their eyes to the
Holy One of Israel.

ISAIAH 17:7

Oceans
to *Enjoy*

THERE'S AN OLD STORY ABOUT a little frog
that was born at the bottom of a small, circular well.
He and his family lived there, and he was content to
play in the water. He thought, *Life doesn't get any bet-*
ter than this. But one day, he climbed to the top of the
well and cautiously peered out over the edge. Lo and
behold, the first thing he saw was a pond a thousand
times bigger than the well. He ventured farther and
discovered a huge lake. Eventually, the little frog
hopped all the way to the ocean, where everywhere
he looked, all he could see was water. He was
shocked beyond measure.

Are you enclosed in your own little well?
Look out over the edge. God has oceans He wants
you to enjoy!

Change Your Family Tree

Tear down your father's altar to Baal and cut down the Asherah pole beside it. Then build a proper kind of altar to the LORD your God on the top of this height.

JUDGES 6:25–26

TOO OFTEN, WE ALLOW complacency to keep us in mediocrity. We get comfortable where we are, and we use that as an excuse. "My parents were poor. Nobody in my family has ever amounted to much, so I guess I won't either."

No, God wants you to go further than your parents ever went. He wants you to break out of that mold. You can do more, have more, be more. You can be the person to change your family tree! Don't pass junk down to your children and keep that negative cycle going. You can break the curse in your family. You can affect future generations by the decisions you make today.

Lord, You have heard the desire of the humble; You will prepare their heart; You will cause Your ear to hear.

PSALM 10:17 NKJV

Let *Faith* Blossom

I KNEW A COUPLE WHO SPENT their days working hard to pay the rent on their small apartment and buy food, while pursuing new opportunities to better themselves. Despite their circumstances, to dream and expand their vision, they dressed up and went to a posh hotel, where they simply sat in the elegant hotel lobby. They looked beyond where they were to where they wanted to be and let faith blossom in their hearts.

Perhaps you, too, need to change your environment. Quit sitting around worrying and feeling sorry for yourself. Instead, go find somewhere you can dream. It may be in a church; it may be along the banks of a stream or at a park. Find someplace where your faith will be elevated.

Soar with Eagles

And Saul's son Jonathan went to David at Horesh and helped him find strength in God.

1 SAMUEL 23:16

*I*T IS AMAZING WHAT CAN HAPPEN when you get into an atmosphere where people build you up rather than tear you down, where people encourage and challenge you to be the best you can be. Spend time with people who inspire you to reach for new heights. If you associate with successful people, before long their enthusiasm will be contagious and you will catch that vision. If you stay in an atmosphere of victory, you will develop a winning mind-set. If you hang around people of faith, your own faith will increase.

It's time for you to soar with the eagles rather than pecking around with the chickens. If you will do your part by continually contemplating the goodness of God, living with faith and expectancy, God will take you places you've never even dreamed of.

How great are his signs, how mighty his wonders! His kingdom is an eternal kingdom; his dominion endures from generation to generation.

DANIEL 4:3

The God of *Increase*

WHEN MY DAD PASSED AWAY and I took over as pastor of Lakewood Church in Houston, people often asked me, "Joel, do you really think you can keep it going? You've got some real big shoes to fill." I understood what they meant, because they loved my dad and he was a great leader. Beyond that, few other churches the size of Lakewood had ever survived for long after the loss of the founding senior pastor.

But none of those matters worried me. I knew God did not desire one generation to shine, and then the next generation to fade into obscurity. God wants each generation to increase. That's just the way our God is. I hope you believe that this morning.

Get *Out* of the Rut

Truly, truly, I say to you, he who believes in Me, the works that I do, he will do also; and greater works than these he will do; because I go to the Father.

JOHN 14:12 NASB

*Y*OU MAY HAVE COME from the wrong family in the wrong part of town. You may not have any money and very little education. In the natural, the future may not look very bright. Some people around you may try to discourage you and tell you there's no reason to hope for more. Others may tell you to stay where it's safe, although it's really being stuck in a rut of defeat and mediocrity.

Don't listen to all the naysayers. Get out of the rut. Don't be satisfied with where you are. God is not limited by your environment, family background, or present circumstances. God is limited only by your lack of faith. Believe Him for the "greater works" He has for you to do. Step out in faith, and you will break through the barriers.

We will not hide them from their children; we will tell the next generation the praiseworthy deeds of the LORD, his power, and the wonders he has done.

PSALM 78:4

Passing on a Legacy

FRIEND, don't ever get satisfied with where you are. Maybe you come from a family like my dad's, where they didn't have much materially. Or maybe you come from a family with tremendous wealth, prestige, and position. Regardless, you can experience more than the generation preceding you.

Respect what your parents accomplished, but don't be satisfied to simply inherit what they have, to do what they did. God wants each generation to go further than the previous generation—to be more blessed, to experience more of His love, goodness, and influence in the world. He doesn't want you to stay where you are. You can be so much more than your predecessors, passing on a legacy of godly attitudes, blessings, and success to your children.

Break the Cycle

"Not by might nor by power, but by my Spirit," says the LORD Almighty.
ZECHARIAH 4:6

MAYBE YOU HAIL FROM a long line of divorce, failure, depression, mediocrity, and other personal or family problems. You need to say, "Enough is enough. I'm going to break out of this cycle and change my expectations. I'm going to start believing God for bigger and better things."

When God puts a dream in your heart, when He brings opportunities across your path, step out boldly in faith, expect the best, move forward with confidence, knowing that you are well able to do what God wants you to do. God wants to do a new thing in your life. What you will receive is directly connected to how you believe. But you've got to do your part and get outside that little box you've grown accustomed to. Start thinking big!

The weapons we fight with are not the weapons of the world. On the contrary, they have divine power to demolish strongholds.

2 CORINTHIANS 10:4

Fresh, *Positive* Attitudes

*I*F YOU DON'T THINK your dreams will ever come to pass, they never will. If you don't think you have what it takes to rise up and set that new standard, it's not going to happen. The barrier is in your mind, which the Scripture calls a "stronghold." It's a wrong thinking pattern that keeps us imprisoned in defeat. And that's why it is so important that we think positive thoughts of hope, faith, and victory.

Perhaps somebody has spoken negative words into your life. Maybe someone has told you that you just don't have what it takes to become successful. Reject those lies wherever you find them. After all, if God is for you, who dares to be against you? Break through those limitations and let your mind dwell on fresh, positive attitudes of faith.

Run *Free*

> But Jesus looked at them and said,
> "With man this is impossible, but with
> God all things are possible."
>
> MATTHEW 19:26

*U*P UNTIL THE EARLY 1950s, track-and-field experts declared that it was impossible for a human being to break the four-minute-mile barrier. But one day a man named Roger Bannister refused to let all those impossibilities form a stronghold in his mind. He began to train, believing he could break the record. And, sure enough, he went out and ran the "Miracle Mile," breaking the four-minute-mile barrier.

Now, here is what is so interesting about this story. Within ten years after Bannister broke the record, 336 more runners also broke it! Think of that. As far back as statisticians kept track-and-field records—hundreds of years—nobody had done it. What changed? Simple. For all those years, the barrier was in the runners' minds. One man proved the experts wrong, and hundreds ran free.

You have dwelt long enough on this mountain. . . . Behold, I have set the land before you; go in and take possession of the land which the Lord swore to your fathers . . . to give to them and to their descendants after them.

DEUTERONOMY 1:6, 8 AMP

Today Is a New Day

WHEN GOD LED the Hebrew people out of slavery in Egypt, the eleven-day journey to the Promised Land took forty years. God wanted them to move forward, but they wandered in the desert, going around the same mountain, time after time. They were trapped in a poor, defeated mentality, focusing on their problems and always complaining about the obstacles.

No matter what you've gone through in the past, no matter how many setbacks you've suffered or who or what has tried to thwart your progress, today is a new day, and God wants to do a new thing in your life. Don't let your past determine your future.

Be a *New* Creation

Therefore, if anyone is in Christ, he is a new creation; the old has gone, the new has come!

2 CORINTHIANS 5:17

$\mathcal{B}$ECAUSE OF THEIR DISOBEDIENCE and lack of faith, the Israelites wandered in the wilderness for forty years. How sad! God had prepared a place of great abundance, a place of great freedom for His people. But they had been beaten down by their oppressors for so long—mistreated and taken advantage of—now, even though God wanted a better life for each of them, they couldn't conceive it.

Do you feel as though you're spinning your wheels in life? Rather than moving forward with an attitude of faith, expecting good things, are you allowing obstacles to stand between you and your destiny? It's time to let go of past hurts, pains, or failures. Refuse to be counted among the doubters. Trust God to lead you in the right direction as you break through the barriers of your past.

Enlarge the place of your tent, and let the curtains of your habitations be stretched out; spare not; lengthen your cords and strengthen your stakes, for you will spread abroad to the right hand and to the left.

ISAIAH 54:2–3 AMP

Think *Twice* as Much

THE BIBLE PROMISES that "instead of your [former] shame" God will give us "a twofold recompense" (Isaiah 61:7 AMP). That means if you'll keep the right attitude, God will pay you back double for your trouble. He'll add up all the injustices, all the pain and abuse that people have caused you, and He'll pay you back with twice as much joy, peace, and happiness. If you will change your thinking, God can change your life.

You were born to win; you were born for greatness; you were created to be a champion in life. Our God is called *El Shaddai*, the God of more than enough. He's not "El Cheapo," the God of barely enough!

Redeemed from the Curse

Christ redeemed us from the curse of the law by becoming a curse for us, for it is written: "Cursed is everyone who is hung on a tree."

GALATIANS 3:13

MAYBE YOU ARE LIVING WITH things that have been in your family for generations—alcoholism, drug addiction, poverty, depression, anger, or low self-esteem. Whatever the problem, the good news is that you can break the cycle. You can choose to rise up and turn the tide with God's help.

God will help you break that curse in your family, but it will take perseverance and a willingness to change your past. Your attitude should be: *This is a new day. I boldly declare we are more than conquerors. It doesn't matter how defeated we have been, how broke we've been, how big our obstacles are, or how powerful our enemies are. Greater is He who is in us than he who is in the world. We are blessed, and we cannot be cursed.*

And we know that in all things God works for the good of those who love him, who have been called according to his purpose.

ROMANS 8:28

God *Will* Open Doors

THE BIBLE CLEARLY STATES that God has crowned us with "glory and honor" (Psalm 8:5). The word *honor* could also be translated as "favor," and *favor* means "to assist, to provide with special advantages and to receive preferential treatment." In other words, God wants to assist you, to promote you, to give you advantages. But to experience more of God's favor, we must live more "favor-minded." We must expect God's special help and release our faith, knowing that God wants to assist us.

We can expect preferential treatment, not because of *who* we are, but because of *whose* we are. It is not because we are better than anybody else or that we deserve it. It is because our Father is the King of kings, and His glory and honor spill over onto us.

Live Favor-Minded

> *So brace up your minds; be sober (circumspect, morally alert); set your hope wholly and unchangeably on the grace (divine favor) that is coming to you when Jesus Christ (the Messiah) is revealed. [Live] as children of obedience [to God]; do not conform yourselves to the evil desires [that governed you] in your former ignorance.*
>
> 1 PETER 1:13–14 AMP

AS GOD'S CHILDREN, we can live with confidence and boldness, expecting good things. If we love God, He's working life to our advantage, and it will all work out for our good, although it may not always be the way we hope. No matter what does or doesn't happen in your life today, keep believing for the favor of God.

Don't take God's favor for granted. Live favor-minded. Get up each day and expect and declare it. Say, "I have the favor of God." Don't sit back passively. You do your part, and God will do His part.

For thou art the glory of their strength: and in thy favour our horn shall be exalted.

PSALM 89:17 KJV

A *Great* Morning

I ONCE MET A MECHANIC who endured unfair compensation practices as well as all sorts of injustice and ridicule from his coworkers for years at a large diesel-truck shop where he worked. He could have grown bitter or quit and found work elsewhere. But instead, he continued to do top-quality work, knowing that he wasn't working to please his supervisor; he was working to please God. One day, the owner of the company called him and said, "I'm ready to retire, and I'm looking for someone I can trust to take over the business and continue the work I've started. I want to give it to you." Today, the mechanic owns that company free and clear!

Isn't this a great morning to start expecting the favor of God to show up in the details of your life?

Perpetual *Forgiveness*

Then Peter came to Jesus and asked, "Lord, how many times shall I forgive my brother when he sins against me? Up to seven times?" Jesus answered, "I tell you, not seven times, but seventy-seven times."

MATTHEW 18:21–22

UNDERSTAND, we serve a God who wants to do more than you can ask or think. Regardless of how people are treating you, keep doing the right thing; don't get offended or upset; don't try to pay them back, returning evil for evil. Instead, keep extending forgiveness; keep responding in love. If you do that, then when it comes time for you to be promoted, God will make sure it happens. He'll make sure you get everything you deserve, and more!

Remember, God can work to bring justice into your life today. Choose today to trust His plan for your life, and start anticipating His touch of favor.

*Your beauty and love chase after me
every day of my life.*

PSALM 23:6 THE MESSAGE

One
Touch
from God

THIS MORNING, if you are living favor-minded, the Bible says, "God's blessings are going to chase you down and overtake you." In other words, you won't be able to outrun the good things of God. Everywhere you go, things are going to change in your favor. Every time you turn around, somebody's going to want to do something good for you. It's all due to the favor of God.

The favor of God comes in the midst of life's challenges. When you are going through tough times, even if your situation looks impossible, stay in an attitude of faith, and start declaring God's favor instead of being discouraged and developing a sour attitude. One touch of God's favor can turn everything around in your life.

Seek God's Favor

The LORD is my portion; I have promised to keep Your words. I sought Your favor with all my heart; be gracious to me according to Your word.

PSALM 119:57–58 NASB

D ECLARING GOD'S FAVOR isn't some spooky, spiritual mumbo-jumbo. It's actually quite easy to declare God's favor in your life. Every morning, say something like this: "Father, I thank You that I have Your favor. Your favor is opening doors of opportunity and bringing success into my life. Your favor is causing people to want to help me." Then go out with confidence, expecting good things to happen, expecting doors to open. There's something special about you. You have the favor of God.

Anytime you get in a situation where you need favor, learn to declare it. You don't have to loudly broadcast it to the world. You can whisper it. The volume of your voice is irrelevant; it's your faith that makes the difference.

*For surely, O LORD, you bless the
righteous; you surround them with
your favor as with a shield.*

PSALM 5:12

Surrounded with Favor

EVEN IN THE MUNDANE ASPECTS OF life, you will not be imposing on God's goodness by declaring His favor. He wants you to act on it. For example, maybe you're stuck in traffic and you are trying to get to an important appointment. Simply declare, "Father, I thank You that I have Your favor, and that You are going to make a way for me where it appears that there is no way right now." Then keep trusting God and looking for the opportunity to open.

Keep in mind that God has your best interests at heart, that He is working everything for your good. Like a good parent, He doesn't always give you what you want. But He always gives you what you need. A delay may be just what you need.

God's *Goodness* Every Day

You have granted me life and favor, and Your care has preserved my spirit.

JOB 10:12 NKJV

WHEN YOU LIVE FAVOR-MINDED, you'll begin to see God's goodness in the everyday, ordinary details at the grocery store, at the ball field, at the mall, at work, or at home. You may be out to lunch when you "just happen" to bump into somebody you've been wanting to meet. Perhaps that person is somebody you admire or hope to learn from, or possibly he or she is someone with whom you have been hoping to do business, but you couldn't get to them. That is not a coincidence. That's the favor of God causing you to be at the right place at the right time.

When those kinds of things happen, be grateful. Be sure to thank God for His favor, and for His special assistance in your life. Don't take God's favor for granted.

In everything he did he had
great success, because the LORD
was with him.

1 SAMUEL 18:14

Speak God's Favor

W E SHOULD GET IN THE HABIT of consistently speaking God's favor over our lives. And not simply over our own lives, but over our businesses, our employees, our children, and our families. Whether you are an accountant, or a lawyer, or a photographer, every day you should say, "Father, I thank You that my clients are loyal to me and want to do business with me." If you work in real estate, you ought to speak God's favor over your property: "Father, I thank You that this property is going to sell. I thank You that Your favor is leading me to the right people who want to buy this home."

Learn to speak God's favor over every area of your life. Remember, the more favor-minded you are, the more of God's favor you're going to experience.

Look for God's Goodness

But seek first his kingdom and his righteousness, and all these things will be given to you as well.

MATTHEW 6:33

A YOUNG WOMAN at Lakewood Church had to have an emergency surgery that wasn't covered by her health insurance. Consequently, she owed the hospital twenty-seven thousand dollars. The hospital worked out a payment plan, which she paid little by little each month, but as a single parent she was really struggling. She didn't complain, though, but rather stayed in an attitude of faith and expectancy, declaring God's favor over her life. She was on the lookout for God's goodness.

Right before Christmas she received a letter from the hospital telling her she had been chosen by the hospital to receive their annual gift. Not only was her debt forgiven but thousands of dollars that she had already paid were refunded. That's the sort of thing that happens "naturally" when we live favor-minded.

Surely goodness and mercy shall follow
me all the days of my life.

PSALM 23:6 NKJV

The *Power*
of God's
Favor

KING DAVID committed adultery with Bath-
sheba and then ordered her husband, Uriah, to be
abandoned in battle, resulting in the man's death.
Nevertheless, the Bible compliments David, saying that he was a man after God's own heart (see
1 Samuel 13:14; Acts 13:22). How could that be?
Because David repented and sought forgiveness,
and God forgave him and gave him a new start.
He didn't focus on his faults or on the things he
had done wrong, but he continued to live favor-
minded, expecting goodness and mercy *all* the
days of his life.

This morning, instead of expecting to get the
short end of the stick in life, why not start expecting
God's blessings to chase after you? Instead of expecting to barely get by in life, start expecting the goodness of God to overtake you.

Help in Times of Need

Noah found favor in the eyes of the LORD.

GENESIS 6:8 NASB

THE FAVOR OF GOD can bring you out of your difficulties and turn your adversities around for good. The Bible is replete with examples of people who were in great need, but then the favor of God came on them in a new way, providing whatever they needed. The whole earth was about to be destroyed by a flood, and God gave Noah the job of building a huge boat, not to mention the gathering of the animals. No doubt, Noah was tempted to get discouraged; yet amazingly, the Bible describes how Noah found favor with God. In other words, God was pleased with Noah, so the favor of God came on him in a fresh, new way, giving him unusual ability. God assisted him, and he was able to build that ark to save his family, the animals, and himself.

God can favor you in the same fresh way.

At this, she bowed down with her face to the ground. She exclaimed, "Why have I found such favor in your eyes that you notice me— a foreigner?"

RUTH 2:10

The *Difference* Maker

*I*F YOU WONDER ABOUT the difference that favor can make in your life, consider Ruth. She was a widow living in a foreign country when the land endured a severe famine. Ruth and her mother-in-law, Naomi, were practically starving to death, so Ruth went out to the fields every day and followed behind the reapers, picking up whatever leftover grain they had missed. Ruth found favor with Boaz, the owner of the field, so Boaz told his workers to leave handfuls of grain on purpose for Ruth. The favor of God came during the crisis, and before long, Ruth and Naomi's circumstances turned around, and their needs were supplied in abundance.

When you are going through tough times, instead of becoming discouraged and developing a sour attitude, more than ever, choose to be favor-minded.

When
Mistreated

> But while Joseph was there in the prison, the LORD was with him; he showed him kindness and granted him favor in the eyes of the prison warden.
>
> GENESIS 39:20–21

OSEPH IS ANOTHER BIBLICAL EXAMPLE of someone who found the favor of God in adversity. He was sold into slavery in Egypt, mistreated, and taken advantage of. But no matter what other people did to him, the Bible repeatedly says that the favor of God was upon Joseph. Even when he was unjustly accused of rape and thrown into prison, he continued to thrive. The favor of God eventually caused him to be released, and he was put in charge of all Egypt's agricultural affairs.

The favor of God came in the midst of a trial, in the midst of life's challenges. When somebody is mistreating you, or you're having financial difficulty, or your whole world is falling apart, expect God's favor to show up. Start this morning.

I would have lost heart, unless I had believed that I would see the goodness of the LORD in the land of the living. Wait on the LORD; be of good courage, and He shall strengthen your heart; wait, I say, on the LORD!

PSALM 27:13–14 NKJV

Never Lose Heart

*I*F YOU WILL LIVE with an attitude of faith, before long God's favor is going to show up, and that difficult situation will turn around to your benefit. The Old Testament character Job went through one of the most trying times any person could ever endure. In less than a year, he lost his family, his business, and his health. He had boils over his entire body and no doubt lived in perpetual pain. But in the midst of that dark hour, Job said to God, "You have granted me life and favor" (Job 10:12 NKJV).

Is it any wonder God restored to Job twice what he had before? Never give up on God.

Never Rule Out God's Favor

Though the fig tree may not blossom, nor fruit be on the vines; though the labor of the olive may fail, and the fields yield no food; though the flock may be cut off from the fold, and there be no herd in the stalls—yet I will rejoice in the LORD, I will joy in the God of my salvation.

HABAKKUK 3:17–18 NKJV

*I*F YOU HAVE READ THE BOOK OF JOB, you realize that although his suffering began in chapter 1, he was not delivered and healed until chapter 42! But from the very beginning, in the darkest moments, Job was saying, "God, I don't care what the situation looks like. You are a good God. Your favor is going to turn this situation around."

Friend, you may be in circumstances today that look impossible, but never rule out the favor of God. Stay in an attitude of faith. God promises that good things will come to you.

Then Jehoahaz sought the LORD's favor, and the LORD listened to him, for he saw how severely the king of Aram was oppressing Israel.

2 KINGS 13:4

Good Things *Will* Come

EVEN IF YOU FEEL YOU are in your darkest hour, boldly declare the favor of God, and nothing can keep you down. The Bible says, "Hope to the end for the divine favor that is coming to you" (see 1 Peter 1:13). Certainly, this verse applies to the future blessings that Christians will receive at the return of Christ. But it is also a present truth. In other words, don't give up. Keep on believing, expecting, declaring. Keep living favor-minded, and God promises that good things will come to you.

If you will keep your hope in the Lord, God says divine favor is coming. You may not be able to see it right now, but when God's favor shows up, things are going to change.

Live the Dream

Cast your cares on the LORD and he will sustain you; he will never let the righteous fall.

PSALM 55:22

I MET A YOUNG WOMAN who described how she lost about two hundred pounds after failing on one diet after another. She said, "One day, I decided to start seeing myself the way I wanted to be—losing the weight and running and playing with my children. I spoke words of victory into my life and said, 'I'm well able to lose this weight. I have discipline and self-control. I'm more than a conqueror.'" Once that new image of herself showed up on the inside, God could easily develop it on the outside. Today she's living out her dream and enjoying a happier, healthier lifestyle.

You must get an image of what you want to be on the inside first, if you want to see it come to pass in your life on the outside.

Then the LORD opened the servant's eyes, and he looked and saw the hills full of horses and chariots of fire all around Elisha.

2 KINGS 6:17

Open My Eyes

WHEN I WAS YOUNG, I often heard my father tell our church congregation, "I want you to look out there with me today and see that brand-new sanctuary." At the time, we were meeting in a small rundown building. But Daddy would say, "I want you to see that new building completed and paid off." People who were visiting with us that particular Sunday probably thought we were crazy. But Daddy would say, "Close your eyes and see that new church sanctuary with me through your eyes of faith. See it full of people worshiping God." We saw that sanctuary many years before it ever came to pass. And today the sixteen-thousand-seat arena of Lakewood Church in Houston has four services each weekend.

Be a big dreamer. Don't make little plans.

Envision Your Dreams

I counsel you to buy from me . . . salve to put on your eyes, so you can see.

REVELATION 3:18

*D*O YOU LOOK UPON your life with eyes of faith? Think of it this way: when we close our eyes, we should see more than we do when we have our eyes open. See your whole family serving God. See yourself rising to new levels of effectiveness. See yourself stronger, healthier, and living a more abundant life. See God using you in a greater way.

Take a few minutes every day to dream big dreams; close your eyes, and envision your dreams coming to pass. Envision yourself out of debt. Envision yourself breaking that addiction. Envision your marriage being more fulfilled. Envision yourself rising to new levels in your career. If you can establish that picture in your heart and mind, then God can begin to bring it to pass in your life.

But by the grace of God I am what I am, and His grace toward me was not in vain.

1 CORINTHIANS 15:10 NKJV

Develop a *Healthy* Self-Image

EVERY PERSON has an image of himself or herself. Psychologists have proven that you will most consistently perform in a manner that is in harmony with the image you have of yourself. If you see yourself as unqualified, unattractive, inferior, or inadequate, you will probably act in accordance with your thoughts. Individuals who view themselves as God sees them are usually happy about who they are. They can honestly say, "Thank You, Father, for creating me the way You did. I'd rather be me than any other person on earth. I know that You have a purpose and a plan for me, and I can't wait to discover it!"

True self-esteem can be based only on what God says about you—not on what you think or feel about yourself. You are who God says you are.

Created in God's Image

Then God said, "Let us make man in our image, in our likeness, and let them rule over the fish of the sea and the birds of the air, over the livestock, over all the earth, and over all the creatures that move along the ground." So God created man in his own image, in the image of God he created him; male and female he created them.

GENESIS 1:26–27

*Y*OUR SELF-IMAGE is much like a self-portrait; it is who and what you picture yourself to be, which may or may not be an accurate reflection of who you really are. How you feel about yourself will have a tremendous impact on how far you go in life, because you will probably speak, act, and react as the person you *think* you are. The truth is, you will never rise above the image you have of yourself in your mind.

This morning, believe you are made in the image of God.

> *Am I now trying to win the approval of men, or of God?... If I were still trying to please men, I would not be a servant of Christ.*
>
> GALATIANS 1:10

Live to *Please* God

CARLY WAS THE LONE WOMAN employed in a largely male-dominated field. She had to earn her right to be heard nearly every day. Overweight, with a halting walk from one leg being slightly shorter than the other, she heard the laughs and snide remarks made behind her back. But Carly knew she was good at what she did, walked past her detractors, receiving one promotion after another, and eventually became the CEO of her company.

Carly's secret is her incredibly positive self-image. She believes that she has been made in the image of God, and that He gives her intrinsic value. She doesn't strive for the approval of others or depend on compliments to feel good about herself. Carly is a living demonstration of how to live your best life now!

God's *Un-conditional* Love

What is man that you are mindful of him, the son of man that you care for him? You made him a little lower than the heavenly beings and crowned him with glory and honor.

PSALM 8:4–5

*G*OD WANTS US TO HAVE healthy, positive self-images, to see ourselves as priceless treasures. He wants us to feel good about ourselves. Despite our faults and weaknesses, God loves us anyway. He created us in His image, and He is continually shaping us, conforming us to His character, helping us to become even more like the person He is.

Consequently, we must learn to love ourselves, faults and all, because that's how our heavenly Father loves us. You can walk with confidence knowing that God loves you unconditionally. His love is based on what you are, not what you do. He created you as a unique individual—there has never been, nor will there ever be, another person exactly like you, and He sees you as His special masterpiece!

The LORD is with you, you mighty man of valor!

JUDGES 6:12 NKJV

Be a *Champion*

*W*HEN THE ANGEL of the Lord appeared to tell Gideon how God wanted him to save the people of Israel from the Midianites, the first words spoken were, "The Lord is with you, you mighty man of [fearless] courage" (Judges 6:12 AMP). Gideon showed his true colors when he replied, "But Lord, how can I save Israel? My clan is the weakest in Manasseh, and I am the least in my family" (v. 15).

Sound familiar? So often, we sense God telling us that He has something big for us to do. But because of a poor self-image, we say, "God, I can't do that. You've got to find somebody more qualified. I don't have what it takes." You may feel unqualified, insecure, weak, fearful, and insignificant, but God sees you as a victor!

When You *Feel* Weak

The LORD turned to him and said, "Go in the strength you have and save Israel out of Midian's hand. Am I not sending you?"

JUDGES 6:14

IT'S INTERESTING TO NOTE the difference between the way Gideon saw himself and the way God rewarded him. Although Gideon felt unqualified, full of fear, and lacking in confidence, God addressed him as a mighty man of fearless courage. Gideon felt weak; God saw him as strong and competent to lead His people into battle and victory. And Gideon did!

Moreover, God sees you as a champion. He believes in you and regards you as a strong, courageous, successful, overcoming person. You may not see yourself that way, but that doesn't change God's image of you. God still sees you exactly as His Word describes you. Learn to love yourself as your heavenly Father loves you.

Keep me as the apple of the eye; hide me in the shadow of Your wings.

PSALM 17:8 NASB

The *Apple* of God's Eye

*D*O YOU KNOW WHO YOU ARE? You are the apple of God's eye. Just as the pupil is in the center of your eye, you are the center of God's attention. You didn't choose God; He chose you. Before you were ever formed in your mother's womb, God saw you. And the Scriptures teach that God has already approved and accepted you. He may not be pleased with every decision you have made, but understand this extremely important truth: God is pleased with you.

If God approves you, why don't you accept and approve yourself? The Scripture doesn't say that God approves you as long as you don't make any mistakes, as long as you don't have any weaknesses. No, God approves you unconditionally. He accepts you and loves you in spite of your faults.

"Good Enough"

Therefore, there is now no condemnation for those who are in Christ Jesus.

ROMANS 8:1

SOMETIMES I SAY OR DO THINGS I wish I wouldn't. Sometimes I have a bad attitude. I may be selfish. But I've learned to ask God's forgiveness for my failures, mistakes, and sins, and move on. I'm not going to go around beating myself up because I'm not perfect. God knows my heart. He knows that at least I'm trying. I've made a decision to hold my head up high and feel good about myself, knowing that God approves of me.

You may have some problem areas you need to overcome, but that's okay. You don't have to go around beating yourself up, living in guilt and condemnation. No, God is in the process of changing you. But if you're constantly at strife within yourself because you feel that you aren't "good enough," your spiritual progress will be thwarted.

The entire law is summed up in a single command: "Love your neighbor as yourself."

GALATIANS 5:14

Love Yourself

SADLY, MANY PEOPLE don't really like themselves. They have a war raging within. They are constantly thinking or speaking negatively about themselves. They feel guilty, inferior, insecure, and condemned. Because of their own self-rejection, they can't get along with other people.

Don't make the mistake of always feeling bad about yourself. God knows you're not perfect and you're going to make some mistakes. You are not surprising God. He made you. He knows everything about you, good and bad, faults and all, and God still loves you. You might as well lighten up a little and learn to love and accept yourself. It's okay to enjoy where you are while God is in the process of changing you and taking you to where He wants you to be.

A *Heart* to Do Right

Then he adds: "Their sins and lawless acts I will remember no more."

HEBREWS 10:17

WE NEED TO NOT BE SO HARD on ourselves when we don't live up to our own unrealistic expectations. "But I can't control my temper," you may say. Or, "I've tried and tried to quit smoking and have failed time after time. God must be just shaking His head in dismay at me."

I'm not saying that it's okay to have a loose attitude toward our mistakes, lack of discipline, or sin. I'm referring to people who have a heart to do what is right, people who are trying to do their best. If that's you, then don't be condemned and live with a heavy heart. The truth is, even after you overcome that bad habit, God will bring another area to light with which you will need to deal. You are a work in progress, and He is constantly changing you for the better.

On this mountain the LORD Almighty will prepare a feast of rich food for all peoples, a banquet of aged wine—the best of meats and the finest of wines.

ISAIAH 25:6

Children of the Most High

SOME PEOPLE LIKE TO remind us that "we're just poor old sinners," but we are sons and daughters of the Most High God. When we came to God, He washed away our sins (see 1 Corinthians 6:9–11). He made us new creatures. The Bible says, "The old things passed away; behold, new things have come" (2 Corinthians 5:17 NASB). He made us the righteousness of God.

Instead of having a poor-old-me mentality, expecting a crumb here and a crumb there, why don't you step up to the dinner table? God has a beautiful banquet in store for you. He has an abundant life for you. You have royal blood flowing through your veins. Your heavenly Father created the whole universe with you in mind.

God's *Grace* Is Sufficient

But he said to me, "My grace is sufficient for you, for my power is made perfect in weakness." Therefore I will boast all the more gladly about my weaknesses, so that Christ's power may rest on me.

2 CORINTHIANS 12:9

GOD LOVES TO USE ORDINARY PEOPLE just like you and me, faults and all, to do extraordinary things. My question to you is: are you allowing your weaknesses and insecurities to keep you from being your best? Are you letting feelings of inadequacy keep you from believing God for bigger things? God wants to use you in spite of your weaknesses. Don't focus on your weaknesses; focus on your God.

You may not feel capable in your own strength, but that's okay. The apostle Paul said, "When I am weak, then I am strong" (2 Corinthians 12:10). God's Word states that He always causes us to triumph in His strength. He expects us to live victoriously.

Now thanks be to God who always leads us in triumph in Christ, and through us diffuses the fragrance of His knowledge in every place.

2 CORINTHIANS 2:14 NKJV

Agree with God

GOD IS NOT PLEASED when we mope around with a "poor me" attitude. When you do that, you're allowing your self-image to be shaped by nonbiblical concepts that are contrary to God's opinions of you. This sort of poor self-image will keep you from exercising your God-given gifts and authority, and it will rob you from experiencing the abundant life your heavenly Father wants you to have.

You can change the image you have of yourself. Start by agreeing with God. Remember, God sees you as strong and courageous, as a man or woman of great honor and valor. He sees you as being more than a conqueror. He has already approved and accepted you. Start seeing yourself as God sees you. Quit making excuses and start stepping out in faith, doing what God has called you to do.

Possess the Land

If God is for us, who can be against us?

ROMANS 8:31

*I*F YOU WERE AMONG the twelve Hebrew spies sent by Moses into Canaan to check out the opposition, what report would you deliver this morning? Ten of the twelve spies came back and said, "It is a land flowing with milk and honey, but there are giants in the land. Moses, *we were in our own sight* as grasshoppers. They're too strong. We'll never defeat them" (see Numbers 13). Compared to the giants, the mental image they had of themselves was as small helpless grasshoppers. The battle was lost before it started.

Joshua and Caleb had a totally different report. "Moses, we are well able to possess the land. Yes, there are giants there, but our God is much bigger. Because of Him, *we are well able*. Let's go in at once and possess the land." Whatever giants you face, make this your confession as well.

*If the LORD is pleased with us, he will
lead us into that land, a land flowing with
milk and honey, and will give it to us.
Only do not rebel against the LORD. And
do not be afraid of the people of the land,
because we will swallow them up. Their
protection is gone, but the LORD is with us.
Do not be afraid of them.*

NUMBERS 14:8–9

Be a "Can Do" Person

JOSHUA AND CALEB saw giants in the Promised Land, believed God, and refused to see themselves as grasshoppers. Instead, they saw themselves
as God's men, led and empowered by God.

What a tremendous truth! We are "well able"
people because our God is so powerful. God wants
you to be a "can do" person—always ready, willing,
and able to do what He commands. Cast down
those negative thoughts and see yourself as God
sees you. Reprogram your mind with God's Word;
change that negative, defeated self-image, and start
seeing yourself as winning.

Guard Your Associations

Do not be misled: "Bad company corrupts good character."

1 CORINTHIANS 15:33

$\mathcal{H}$OW DO YOU SEE YOURSELF? Do you see yourself as successful? Healthy? Upbeat? Happy? Do you see yourself as being used by God? Do you see yourself as "well able" to do what God wants you to do, strong in the Lord and the power of His might? Or have you allowed yourself to adopt a mentality that says, "I'll never make it in life. My dreams will never come to pass. My marriage is too far gone. I'm too far in debt. I'll never get out of the hole I'm in."

Beware of associating with or adopting the attitudes of people who, through their negative outlook and lack of self-esteem, will rob you of the greatness that God has for you. God wants you to accomplish great things in life, and He's put incredible potential, gifts, and talents within you to enable you to do so.

I have loved you with an everlasting love; I have drawn you with loving-kindness.

JEREMIAH 31:3

Claim *Your* Birthright

MY DAD WAS RAISED IN AN extremely poor cotton-picking family, who lost everything they owned during the Great Depression. He said that from the moment he gave his heart to God at the age of seventeen, "I made a quality decision that my children and family would never have to experience the lack that I was raised in." He searched the Scripture to see what God said about him and started seeing himself not as a farmer's child with no future but as a child of the Most High God. He rose up and broke the curse of poverty in our family.

No wonder my dad held up his Bible every service and said, "This is my Bible. I am what it says I am. I have what it says I have." Do the same this morning, and you'll be amazed what can happen.

Put on God's Approval

Stand firm then, with the belt of truth buckled around your waist, with the breastplate of righteousness in place.

EPHESIANS 6:14

IN THE LIVING BIBLE, Ephesians 6:14 says, "You will need . . . the breastplate of God's approval." Every morning, no matter how you feel or what you may have done wrong the day before, you can get up and say, "Father, I thank You that I'm forgiven. I thank You that You approve me and that I am your friend."

If you'll do that, you'll be amazed at what begins to happen. Your whole self-image will change. That heavy load of guilt and condemnation will be lifted off you. You'll get your joy back. You'll go out to meet the day with a whole new attitude. But it does not happen automatically; it is something we must do. Just as we put on our clothes every morning, we need to get up and consciously put on God's approval.

The righteous are bold as a lion.

PROVERBS 28:1 NASB

As *Bold* as a Lion

DON'T ALLOW A BLACK CLOUD to follow you around. Shake off that sense of unworthiness. You may be dealing with a lot of faults. But remember, God is still working on you. You may not be all you want to be, but at least you can thank God you're not what you used to be. Stop looking at how far you have to go, and take a look at how far you've already come.

God sees the person you are capable of becoming. He's not focused on what you are today; He's focused on your possibilities and what you can become—a lion. To God, you are a diamond in the rough. You may need a lot of polishing. That's okay; we all do. But God will keep working on you and making you into the person He wants you to be.

Something Greater

Jesus looked at him and said, "You are Simon son of John. You will be called Cephas" (which, when translated, is Peter).

JOHN 1:42

WHEN FIRST CALLED BY JESUS, Simon was presumptuous, opinionated, hotheaded, and self-centered—not to mention he sometimes used profane language. Why did God choose him? Because God looks at the heart. Man looks on the outside, but God looks deep down into a person and sees what a person can become. In changing his name to Peter, Jesus meant, "When I get through with you, you're going to be something much greater."

In the same way, God has put more in you than you can even imagine. You have gifts and talents that nobody else has. God has planted seeds of greatness in you. Why don't you quit looking at what you can't do and start looking at what God can do? It's not where you are that matters; it's where God can take you.

Like clay in the hand of the potter, so are you in my hand, O house of Israel.

JEREMIAH 18:6

In *Good* Hands

ONE DAY THE master artist Michelangelo was working on a huge rock with his hammer and chisel, in the beginning stages of sculpting it into a piece of art. He knew it was going to be a long, drawn-out process. Somebody came along and asked, "Why are you wasting your time on that ugly rock?" Michelangelo said, "I see a beautiful angel trapped in this rock, and I'm doing my best to let him out."

And that's exactly the way God sees us. You may feel that you are nothing more than a useless lump of rock. But when God looks at you, He sees a valuable son or daughter whom He created in His own image. He's chipping away, knocking off the rough, unsightly edges, molding you, shaping you, until He gets the angel out of the rock.

Do *Your* Part

For it is by grace you have been saved, through faith—and this not from yourselves, it is the gift of God.

EPHESIANS 2:8

GOD IS A GOD OF SECOND CHANCES—and third, and fourth, and even more chances. He loves you. God's approval is not based on your achievements. It is based solely on the fact that you are His child and He sees the best in you. There's nothing you can do, and there's nothing anybody else can do, that will ever change your value in God's eyes.

But you have to do your part. Quit over-analyzing your faults; stop taking an inventory of everything wrong with you. If you make mistakes, ask for forgiveness and then move on. Don't become overly concerned if you are not changing as quickly as you would like. Stay focused on what you can become, and God will get you to where you need to be.

And I am convinced and sure of this very thing, that He Who began a good work in you will continue until the day of Jesus Christ [right up to the time of His return], developing [that good work] and perfecting and bringing it to full completion in you.

PHILIPPIANS 1:6 AMP

Made with *Great* Value

AN IMPORTANT FACTOR in seeing yourself God's way is to understand your intrinsic sense of value. Your sense of value cannot be based on your successes or failures, how somebody else treats you, or how popular you are. It is not something we earn; indeed, we cannot earn it. God built value into us when He created us.

As His unique creation, you have something to offer this world that nobody else has, that nobody else can be. Your sense of value should be based solely on the fact that you are a child of the Most High God. Learn to be happy with who God made you to be.

From Glory to *Glory*

But we all, with open face beholding as in a glass the glory of the Lord, are changed into the same image from glory to glory, even as by the Spirit of the Lord.

2 CORINTHIANS 3:18 KJV

THE SCRIPTURE SAYS "we are God's workmanship" (Ephesians 2:10), which implies that you are a "work in progress." Throughout our lives, God is continually shaping us into the people He wants us to be. The key to future success is to not be discouraged about your past or present while you are in the process of being "completed."

God loves you unconditionally. You may not understand everything you are going through right now. But hold your head high, knowing that God is in control and He has a great plan and purpose for your life. Your dreams may not have turned out exactly as you'd hoped, but the Bible says that God's ways are better and higher than our ways.

No power in the sky above or in the earth below—indeed, nothing in all creation will ever be able to separate us from the love of God that is revealed in Christ Jesus our Lord.

ROMANS 8:39 NLT

Unchanging *Value*

THIS MORNING, imagine that I am handing you a new, crisp one-hundred-dollar bill. Would you want it? Probably so! If I crumpled it, you'd still want it. And if I threw it on the ground and stomped on it until the picture on the bill was barely perceptible, you'd still want it, because you know that a beat-up hundred-dollar bill is still worth a hundred dollars.

That's the way God sees each of us. We all go through challenges and struggles. Sometimes we feel like that crumpled and soiled hundred-dollar bill. But, in fact, we will never, ever lose our value, which has been placed in us by the Creator of the universe. Nobody can take it away from us.

His Very Own Child

Even if my father and mother abandon me, the LORD will hold me close.

PSALM 27:10 NLT

*U*NFORTUNATELY, you may have gone through some traumatic, painful experiences in which somebody mistreated you, used you, or rejected you. Maybe your husband or wife walked out on you or a good friend turned on you for no reason. Or maybe you felt rejected as a child, and you are living with feelings of heartache, pain, guilt, and condemnation. Perhaps you've even convinced yourself that the negative things that happened in your past are all your fault.

Friend, nothing could be further from the truth. You cannot allow your self-esteem and your sense of value to be determined by how other people treat you. God accepts us even if everybody else in this world rejects us. He will take you in and adopt you as His very own child.

He lifted me out of the slimy pit, out of the mud and mire; he set my feet on a rock and gave me a firm place to stand. He put a new song in my mouth, a hymn of praise to our God.

PSALM 40:2–3

Sing a *New* Song

MAYBE YOU LIVE OR WORK with somebody who is always putting you down and criticizing you. Let that misinformation go in one ear and out the other. Constantly remind yourself that you are made in the image of Almighty God and crowned with glory and honor. Don't let other people play games with your mind, deceiving you into thinking that your value is diminished.

God wants to put a new song in your heart; He wants to fill you with hope. He wants you to know that He loves you more than you can imagine, and He can turn your dashed dreams into something beautiful.

Change What You Expect

*Listen to my voice in the morning,
LORD. Each morning I bring my
requests to you and wait expectantly.*

PSALM 5:3 NLT

OUR EXPECTATIONS WIELD a tremendous power in our lives. We don't always get what we deserve in life, but we usually get no more than we expect; we receive what we believe. Unfortunately, this principle works as strongly in the negative as it does in the positive. Many people expect defeat, failure, and mediocrity, and they usually get it.

But you can believe for good things just as easily as you can expect the worst. The key is to expect good things from God. When you encounter tough times, ask God for wisdom, and change what you expect. Even if the bottom falls out of your life, your attitude should be: *God, I know that You are going to use this for my good. I believe that You're going to bring me out stronger than ever before.*

If you do not stand firm in your faith, you will not stand at all.

ISAIAH 7:9

Firm in Your Faith

UNDERSTAND THIS: GOD WILL help you in life, but you cast the deciding vote. If you choose to stay focused on negative elements in your life, if you focus on what you can't do and what you don't have, then by your own choice you are agreeing to be defeated. You are conspiring with the enemy by opening the door and allowing destructive thoughts, words, actions, and attitudes to dominate your life.

However, if you'll get into agreement with God, if you'll focus on your possibilities, your faith can cause God to show up and work supernaturally in your life. But it's up to you. It depends on your outlook. Consider this: you are today what you believed about yourself yesterday. And you will be tomorrow what you believe about yourself right now.

Become What *You* Believe

> *But He said, "The things which are impossible with men are possible with God."*
>
> LUKE 18:27 NKJV

*P*ERHAPS THIS morning you are saying, "Joel, I don't want to get my hopes up. I've prayed. I've done everything I know to do. Nothing's changed. If I don't get my hopes up and nothing good happens to me, at least I won't be disappointed."

Friend, you *must* get your hopes up, or you won't have faith. Consider the fascinating account of two blind men who heard that Jesus was passing by. When Jesus heard their cries for mercy, He posed an intriguing question: "Do you believe that I am able to do this?" (Matthew 9:28 NASB). Jesus wanted to know whether they had genuine faith. The blind men answered, "Yes, Lord; we believe." Then the Bible says, "[Jesus] touched their eyes and said, 'Become what you believe'" (v. 29 THE MESSAGE). What a powerful statement about their faith! *You will become what you believe!*

[God said to Abraham,] "I will bless you and make your name famous, and you will be a blessing to many others."

GENESIS 12:2 TLB

According to *Your* Faith

*I*N MATTHEW 9, after the two blind men told Jesus they believed He was able to heal them, the Bible says, "Then He touched their eyes, saying, According to your faith and trust and reliance [on the power invested in Me] be it done to you; and their eyes were opened" (vv. 29–30 AMP). Notice, it was their faith that brought them the healing.

What are you believing? Are you believing to go higher in life, to rise above your obstacles, to live in health, abundance, healing, and victory? You will become what you believe. You don't have to figure out how God is going to solve your problems or bring it to pass. That's His responsibility. Your job is to believe. Your faith will help you overcome your obstacles.

A Life Filled with *Love*

When you open your hand, they are satisfied with good things.

PSALM 104:28

WHEN TIMES GET TOUGH—as they often do—or things don't go your way—as they sometimes don't—keep on believing in God. When discouragements come, or when people tell you that your dreams are never going to come to pass, boldly remind yourself that God is opening doors of opportunity for you.

God doesn't want you to drag through life, barely making it. Dare today to start believing God for greater things. Dare to believe Him for a better marriage, for better health, for increase and abundance. God wants you to have a good life, a life filled with love, joy, peace, and fulfillment. That doesn't mean it will always be easy, but it does mean it will always be good. God causes all things to work together for good to those who love Him (see Romans 8:28).

Surely the arm of the LORD is not too short to save, nor his ear too dull to hear.

ISAIAH 59:1

Keep *Hope* Alive

*M*AYBE YOU HAVE ENDURED unspeakable negative things, to the point that you have lost your dreams. You are drifting through life, taking whatever comes your way. You may be tempted to tell yourself, "I've been living this way too long. I'm never going to get any better. I've prayed, I've believed, I've done everything I know how to do. Nothing's worked. My life is in too big of a mess; you can't unscramble eggs," and that is true. But God can take scrambled eggs and make an amazing omelet.

Friend, if you don't have faith, you can't please God, and you won't see His power revealed in your life. No matter how many setbacks you've suffered, God still has a great plan for your life. Keep hope alive in your heart. Never give up on your dreams.

Fight the *Good* Fight

> *"No weapon forged against you will prevail, and you will refute every tongue that accuses you. This is the heritage of the servants of the LORD, and this is their vindication from me,"* declares the LORD.
>
> ISAIAH 54:17

MAKE NO MISTAKE ABOUT IT, there will be opposition in your life; there will be weapons formed against you, and they may be formidable and frightening. You will not go under; you will go through. The Scripture says, "A righteous man may have many troubles, but the LORD delivers him from them all" (Psalm 34:19).

When things get tough or things don't go your way, keep your confidence up. The Bible says when you've done all you know how to do, just keep on standing strong. Keep praying, keep believing, keep singing songs of praise. Keep fighting the good fight. If you do that, God promises to bring you out with the victory.

By faith he left Egypt, not fearing the king's anger; he persevered because he saw him who is invisible.

HEBREWS 11:27

Seeing the Invisible

THE WORLD TELLS YOU, "You need to see it to believe it." But God says, "[Faith] is the confident assurance that what we hope for is going to happen. It is the evidence of things we cannot yet see" (Hebrews 11:1 NLT). Only as you believe it will you ever see it. Once you see it by faith, it can come into existence in the physical world.

Begin this morning to believe that what you have hoped for is going to happen, that good things are on their way. You may have all kinds of problems, and in the natural order, it doesn't look as though anything is turning around. But don't be discouraged. Look into that invisible world, into the supernatural world, and through your eyes of faith, see that situation turning around. See your joy and peace being restored.

The *Key* to the Promise

So Sarah laughed to herself as she thought, "After I am worn out and my master is old, will I now have this pleasure?"

GENESIS 18:12

*I*T WAS NEARLY TWENTY YEARS after God first spoke the promise to Abraham that he and his wife, Sarah, were going to have a child that Isaac was born. When Sarah heard the promise again, she and Abraham were close to one hundred years old, and she laughed. She probably said, "Abraham, that's impossible. I'm too old." Nevertheless, Sarah became pregnant. What changed? I'm convinced that the key to the promise's coming to pass was that Sarah had to believe it in her heart before she could become pregnant. And I believe the main reason Isaac wasn't born sooner was simply the fact that Sarah couldn't see it through her eyes of faith.

Do you have a promise from God that is waiting for you to believe?

I came that they may have and enjoy life, and have it in abundance (to the full, till it overflows).

JOHN 10:10 AMP

Abundance in Life

WHEN YOU READ JESUS' PROMISE IN John 10, is your first thought all the reasons why it can't happen to you? "God, I've got too many things wrong with me to ever be healthy. I'm not gifted, and I've never graduated from college, so I can't be prosperous. I'm too old. I'm too young. I'm the wrong sex. My skin is the wrong color." All that time, God is trying to plant the new seed of victory inside us. He's trying to get us to conceive it in our hearts through faith, so it will come to pass.

Friend, God is not limited to the laws of nature. If you'll let that seed take root so it can grow, putting your trust and confidence in the Lord, God will do the impossible.

The *Price* Has Been Paid

You were bought at a price; do not become slaves of men.

1 CORINTHIANS 7:23

THERE WAS A MAN who traveled across the Atlantic on a cruise ship but never ate in the dining room. Instead, he would go off in a corner and eat cheese and crackers he had brought with him. Near the end of the trip, another man asked him, "Why don't you come into the banquet hall and eat with us?" The traveler's face flushed with embarrassment. "Well, to tell you the truth, I had only enough money to buy the ticket." The other passenger shook his head and said, "Sir, the meals were included in the price of the ticket!"

Many of us are missing out on God's best because we don't realize that the good things in life have already been paid for in our redemption. We are surviving on cheese and crackers, while God has made much more available to us in Christ.

O taste and see that the LORD is good; how blessed is the man who takes refuge in Him!

PSALM 34:8 NASB

Come to the *Banquet*

OO MANY OF US GO THROUGH LIFE with a weak worm-of-the-dust mentality. Every time we shrink back and say, "Well, I can't do it; I don't have what it takes," we're conforming to it. When we allow ourselves to be full of fear, worry, or anxiety, or when we are uptight about something, we're surrendering to a worm mentality.

It's time to step up to God's dining table and dig in to the fabulous banquet He has prepared for you, complete with every good thing imaginable. God has everything you need—joy, forgiveness, restoration, peace, healing—anything you need to live at your full potential. It's all waiting for you at God's banquet table, if you'll pull up your chair and take the place He has prepared for you. Best of all, the price has already been paid.

Eyes of Faith

Praise be to the God and Father of our Lord Jesus Christ, who has blessed us in the heavenly realms with every spiritual blessing in Christ.

EPHESIANS 1:3

ONE OF THE MOST IMPORTANT aspects of seeing ourselves God's way involves developing a prosperous mind-set. Understand, God has already equipped you with everything you need to live a prosperous life and to fulfill your God-given destiny. He planted "seeds" inside you filled with possibilities, incredible potential, creative ideas, and dreams. But you have to start tapping into them.

You've got to believe beyond a shadow of a doubt that you have what it takes. God created you to excel, and He's given you ability, insight, talent, wisdom, and His supernatural power to do so. This morning, God has everything you need. Enter into the joy of the Lord and be faithful to use all He's given you.

No, in all these things we are more
than conquerors through him
who loved us.

ROMANS 8:37

More than Conquerors

*N*OTICE THAT THE APOSTLE PAUL did not say we will become conquerors; he says we are more than conquerors *right now*. If you will start acting like it, talking like it, seeing yourself as more than a conqueror, you will live a prosperous and victorious life. The price has already been paid for you to have joy, peace, and happiness. That's part of the package that God has made available to you.

Start looking through eyes of faith, seeing yourself rising to new levels. See yourself prospering, and keep that image in your heart and mind. You may be living in poverty at the moment, but don't ever let poverty live in you. The Bible shows that God takes pleasure in prospering His children. As His children prosper spiritually, physically, and materially, their increase brings God pleasure.

Honor His Great Name

My God will supply all your needs according to His riches in glory in Christ Jesus.

PHILIPPIANS 4:19 NASB

*M*Y FATHER GREW UP with a "poverty mentality," and for years in the ministry, he thought he was doing God a favor by staying poor. God tried to bless and increase my dad, but he couldn't receive it. Later, Daddy learned that as God's children, we are able to live an abundant life; that we should even expect to be blessed. Indeed, it is as important to learn how to receive a blessing as it is to be willing to give one.

If I introduced my children to you with shabby clothes and no shoes, their poverty would be a direct reflection on me as their dad. Similarly, when we go through life with a poverty mentality, it is does not honor God's great name. He wants to supply every need you have, and He will!

Mephibosheth bowed down and said, "What is your servant, that you should notice a dead dog like me?"

2 SAMUEL 9:8

How Low Can *You* Go?

WHAT A TRAGEDY IT WOULD BE to go through life as a child of the King in God's eyes, yet as a lowly pauper in our own eyes. That is precisely what happened to Mephibosheth after his grandfather, King Saul, and father, Jonathan, were killed in battle. Fleeing the palace, Mephibosheth became crippled as a result of a fall and was taken to Lodebar, a poverty-stricken city where he lived almost his entire life in terrible conditions. Years later, David, who succeeded Saul as king, ordered Mephibosheth to be brought to live in the palace and treated as royalty.

Despite being royalty and the fact that his father was in a covenant relationship with David, Mephibosheth settled for poverty because he saw himself as a loser and outcast. His life was transformed instantly, but think of all the years he wasted.

Covenant Love

David asked, "Is there anyone still left of the house of Saul to whom I can show kindness for Jonathan's sake?"

2 SAMUEL 9:1

MEPHIBOSHETH WAS THE GRANDSON of the king, but his inner view of himself kept him from receiving the privileges that rightfully belonged to him. Are you doing something similar? Is your self-image so contrary to the way God sees you that you are missing out on God's best? God sees you as a champion. You see yourself as a dead dog.

Maybe you've been hurt in life or made some wrong choices. But if you have honestly repented and done your best to do right since then, you no longer have to live with guilt and shame. You may be crippled physically, spiritually, or emotionally. That does not change God's covenant with you. You are still a child of the Most High God. He has great things in store for you. Be bold and claim what belongs to you.

> You prepare a table before me in the presence of my enemies; You anoint my head with oil; my cup runs over.
>
> PSALM 23:5 NKJV

The *Table* Is Prepared

OW WOULD YOU FEEL if you prepared a delicious dinner and spread the food out on the table, but your children come in, refuse to sit at the table, and instead crawl under the table and wait for some scraps or crumbs to fall? For whatever reason, they don't feel good enough to sit at the table and enjoy the food as well as your company.

Friend, do you want to make your heavenly Father happy? Then start stepping up to the dinner table and enjoying His blessings. You don't have to live in guilt and condemnation any longer; you don't have to go through life full of fear and worry. The price has been paid. Come into the banquet hall and take your rightful place as His child.

No Pretending

Don't copy the behavior and customs of this world, but let God transform you into a new person by changing the way you think. Then you will learn to know God's will for you, which is good and pleasing and perfect.

ROMANS 12:2 NLT

$\mathcal{S}$OME PEOPLE ARE OUTGOING and energetic; others are more timid and laid-back. Some people like to wear suits and ties; other people are more comfortable wearing blue jeans. Some people close their eyes and lift their hands when they worship God; others worship God in a more subdued manner. And God likes it all!

Don't think that you have to fit into somebody else's mold; and, similarly, don't be upset when other people don't fit into your mold. Your attitude should be: *I am confident in who I am. I'm not going to go around pretending, wishing I were something else, trying to fit into everybody's mold.*

Each one should test his own actions.
Then he can take pride in himself,
without comparing himself to some-
body else, for each one should carry
his own load.

GALATIANS 6:4–5

Dare to Be *Happy*

DARE TO BE HAPPY WITH who you are this morning. Many social, physical, and emotional problems stem from the fact that people don't like themselves. They are uncomfortable with how they look, how they talk, or how they act. They don't like their personality. They are always comparing themselves with other people, wishing they were something different.

You were created to be you. If God had wanted you to look like anyone else, He would have made you look like them. If God had wanted you to have a different personality, He would have given you that personality. Be happy with who God made you to be, and quit wishing you were something different.

Be an Original

I know the LORD is always with me. I will not be shaken, for he is right beside me.

PSALM 16:8 NLT

YOU WERE NOT CREATED TO MIMIC somebody else. God doesn't want a bunch of clones. He likes variety, and you should not let people pressure you or make you feel badly about yourself because you don't fit their image of who you should be. You don't need anybody else's approval. God has given us all different gifts, talents, and personalities on purpose. When you go around trying to be like somebody else, not only does it demean you, it steals your uniqueness.

Be an original, not a copycat. Dare to be different; be secure in who God made you to be and then go out and be the best you that you can be. If you run the race and be the best that you can be, then you can feel good about yourself.

Do you not know that in a race all the runners run, but only one gets the prize? Run in such a way as to get the prize.

1 CORINTHIANS 9:24

Run Your Own Race

I ONCE HEARD A MINISTER TELL how he got out of bed every day at 4:00 a.m. and prayed for two hours. My first reaction was, "Oh, my. I don't pray for two hours a day, and I don't get up that early." The more I thought about it, the worse I felt! Finally, I had to say, "That's great for him, but it's not great for me! I'm going to run my race, and I'm not going to compare myself to others."

God has an individual plan for each of our lives. If we make the mistake of trying to copy other people, we're going to waste a lot of time and energy. Worse yet, we may miss the good things God has for us to do.

Live to *Please* God

To the man who pleases him, God gives wisdom, knowledge and happiness.

ECCLESIASTES 2:26

GOD HAS GIVEN YOU the grace to do what He's called you to do. He has not given you the grace to do what everybody else is doing. Take care of yourself; quit looking at what everybody else is doing. Be your best, regardless of whether you come in first or last, whether you get the big promotion or not, whether you make the grade or fall on your face in failure. If you do, you can hold your head high.

Granted, you will face enormous pressure to do what everybody else is doing, to try to please everybody and meet all their expectations. Accept the fact that everybody's not going to agree with every decision you make. But you don't have to please everyone else; you need to please only God.

For by wise counsel you will wage your own war, and in a multitude of counselors there is safety.

PROVERBS 24:6 NKJV

Seek *Wise* Counsel

*I*F YOU FACE DIFFICULT DECISIONS, it helps to seek counsel from someone you respect. We should always stay open and be willing to take advice. But after you've prayed about something and looked at all the options, be bold enough to make a decision that is right for you. If you're trying to please everybody else by doing things you don't really want to do, you will be cheating yourself. You can run yourself in circles trying to be something that you're not, and you'll run the risk of missing out on God's best for your own life.

Make sure the people who are giving you advice have earned your respect as a source of wisdom. Then, you need to follow your own heart in light of God's Word and do what you feel is right and good for you.

Your Time to *Shine*

Have I not commanded you? Be strong and courageous! Do not tremble or be dismayed, for the LORD your God is with you wherever you go.

JOSHUA 1:9 NASB

WHEN MOSES DIED, God selected Joshua to take over as leader of His people. God said to Joshua, "Just as I have been with Moses, I will be with you" (Joshua 1:5 NASB). Notice He didn't say, "Joshua, be just like Moses, then you'll be okay." No, God said to Joshua, "Be who I made you to be, and then you'll be successful."

And that's all He expects of you, as well. You may have some faults, some areas you and God are refining. But remember, God is in the process of changing you. And if you will choose to be happy with who God made you to be, and make a decision that today you're going to be the best you can be, God will pour out His favor in your life.

This is what the LORD says—he who created you, O Jacob, he who formed you, O Israel: "Fear not, for I have redeemed you; I have summoned you by name; you are mine."

ISAIAH 43:1

Don't Copy Anyone

WHEN I BECAME THE SENIOR PASTOR at Lakewood Church, I was concerned about how I was going to be accepted. After all, my dad had been in that position for forty years, and his style and personality were much different from mine. He was a fireball of a preacher; I'm much more laid-back. One night I was asking God, "Should I try to be more like my dad? Should I copy his style?" But the Lord spoke deep down in my heart, saying, "Joel, don't copy anybody. Be who I created you to be. I don't want a duplicate of your dad. I want an original." That truth set me free!

If you are trying to be what everybody else wants you to be, it's time to stop. Be who you are.

The *Power* of Thoughts and Words

The mind of sinful man is death, but the mind controlled by the Spirit is life and peace.

ROMANS 8:6

A POWERFUL STEP TOWARD LIVING at your full potential is to discover the power of your thoughts and words. Many people are not reaching their full potential because their thinking patterns are defective. You cannot think negative thoughts and expect to live a positive life. You can't think thoughts of failure and expect to succeed.

You've got to quit dwelling on the negative. Don't magnify your problems. Magnify your God. The bigger we make God, the smaller our problems become. Quit dwelling on what's wrong in your life, and start dwelling on what's right in your life. Learn to focus on your possibilities, on what you can do, on your potential. Then go out each day expecting good things. Friend, if you are going to live your best life now, you must learn how to control your thought life.

You will keep in perfect peace him whose mind is steadfast, because he trusts in you.

ISAIAH 26:3

Battles in the Mind

WHETHER OR NOT you are aware of it, a war is raging all around you, and the battle is for your mind. Your enemy's number one target is the arena of your thoughts. If he can control how you think, he'll be able to control your entire life. Indeed, thoughts determine actions, attitudes, and self-image. Really, thoughts determine destiny, which is why the Bible warns us to guard our minds.

Don't ever start your day in neutral. This morning, set your mind on the right course by agreeing with the psalmist: "This is the day the Lord has made, and I'm going to be happy. I'm going to go out and be productive. This is going to be a great day." Magnify your God, and go out each day expecting good things.

Success Begins in the Mind

This is what the LORD says to you: "Do not be afraid or discouraged because of this vast army. For the battle is not yours, but God's."

2 CHRONICLES 20:15

EVERY MORNING, when you first get up, set your mind for success. Almost like a magnet, we draw in what we constantly think about, and it becomes a battlefield in our mind. If we dwell on depressing, negative thoughts, we will be depressed and negative. If we think positive, happy, joyful thoughts, our life will reflect that and attract other upbeat, positive people. Our life follows our thoughts.

And our thoughts also affect our emotions. We will feel exactly the way we think. You cannot expect to feel happy unless you think happy thoughts. Conversely, it's impossible to remain discouraged unless you first think discouraging thoughts. So much of success and failure in life begins in our minds.

Since, then, you have been raised with Christ, set your hearts on things above, where Christ is seated at the right hand of God.

COLOSSIANS 3:1

First *Change* Your Thinking

HEAR PEOPLE SAY, "I never get any breaks. Nothing good ever happens to me. I knew I wasn't going to get that promotion." Unfortunately, they get exactly what they expect. "But you don't understand," you may be saying. "My health is going downhill," or "My marriage is not what it should be," or "I'm having so many financial problems."

Friend, your life is not going to change until you first change your thinking. You may be in negative circumstances today; you may have unfair things happening to you. But don't make the mistake of dwelling on those things. You've got to get your mind moving in a new, positive direction. Don't wait to see what kind of day it's going to be before you decide whether you're going to be positive. Set your mind now!

Think about *Your* Thinking

Let this mind be in you which was also in Christ Jesus.

PHILIPPIANS 2:5 NKJV

*L*IFE IS TOUGH. We all get knocked down occasionally and get discouraged, but we need not remain there. We can choose our thoughts. Nobody can make us think a certain way. If you're not happy, nobody is forcing you to be unhappy. If you're negative and have a bad attitude, nobody's coercing you to be sarcastic or sullen. You decide what you will entertain in your mind.

Simply because the enemy plants a negative, discouraging thought in your brain doesn't mean you have to nurture and help it grow. If you do, though, that thought will affect your emotions, your attitudes, and eventually your actions. You will be much more prone to discouragement and depression, and if you continue pondering that negative thought, it will sap the energy and strength right out of you. Choose to believe that God is greater than your problems.

Commit to the Lord whatever you do, and your plans will succeed.

PROVERBS 16:3

Reject the Garbage

*Y*OUR MIND IS SIMILAR TO a computer in that your brain stores every thought you've ever had. That's encouraging when you're trying to find your car keys, but it's not such good news when you consider the amount of smut, foul language, ungodly concepts, and other negative input with which we are inundated every day. Nevertheless, simply because a destructive thought is stored in your mental computer does not mean we have to pull it up and run it on the main screen of our minds. The more we dwell on the enemy's lies, the more garbage we willingly allow him to dump into our minds.

What are you allowing your mind to dwell on? Are you constantly contemplating negative things? How you view life makes all the difference in the world—especially for you!

Live *Without* Excuses

You'll do best by filling your minds and meditating on things true, noble, reputable, authentic, compelling, gracious—the best, not the worst; the beautiful, not the ugly; things to praise, not things to curse.

PHILIPPIANS 4:8 THE MESSAGE

WE MUST TAKE RESPONSIBILITY for our minds and our actions. As long as we keep making excuses and blaming our family tree, our environment, past relationships with other people, and our circumstances, and attributing blame to God, Satan, *anyone*, or *anything*, we will never be truly free and emotionally healthy. To a large extent, we can control our own destinies.

It's not your circumstances that have you down; your *thoughts* about your circumstances have you down. It is possible to be in one of the biggest battles for your life and still be filled with joy and peace and victory—if you simply learn how to choose the right thoughts. Fill your mind with God's Word.

As he thinks within himself, so he is.

PROVERBS 23:7 NASB

As You *Think*, You Will Be

*I*T IS UNREALISTIC TO PRETEND that nothing bad ever happens to us. Bad things happen to good people. Pretense is not the answer; nor is playing semantic games to make yourself sound more spiritual. If you are sick, admit it; but keep your thoughts on your Healer. If your body is tired, if your spirit is weary, fine; but focus your thoughts on the One who has promised, "Those who wait on the LORD shall renew their strength" (Isaiah 40:31 NKJV).

Jesus said, "In the world you will have tribulation; but be of good cheer, I have overcome the world" (John 16:33 NKJV). He wasn't saying that troublesome times wouldn't come; He was saying that when they do, we can choose our attitudes. We can choose to believe and dwell on the promises of God's Word.

Propelled Toward *Greatness*

Do not be anxious about anything, but in everything, by prayer and petition, with thanksgiving, present your requests to God. And the peace of God, which transcends all understanding, will guard your hearts and your minds in Christ Jesus.

PHILIPPIANS 4:6–7

*I*F WE ARE GOING TO BECOME all God wants us to be, we must win the victory in our own minds. You can't sit back passively and expect this new person to suddenly appear. If you don't think you can be successful, you never will be. If you don't think your body can be healed, it never will be. When you think thoughts of mediocrity, you are destined to live an average life.

But when you align your thoughts with God's thoughts and start dwelling on the promises of His Word, when you constantly dwell on thoughts of His victory and favor, you will be propelled toward greatness, inevitably bound for increase, promotion, and God's supernatural blessings.

What I fear comes upon me,
and what I dread befalls me.

JOB 3:25 NASB

Don't Give Fear a Thought

THE OLD TESTAMENT STORY of Job has many lessons for us, but one especially powerful principle is revealed early in the calamities that came upon that good man. He lamented that what he feared had come upon him. When good people agree with the enemy, he is given the right to bring bad things into being. When people spew a litany of fear-filled ideas in their daily conversations, such as "I'm afraid my business is never going to grow" or "I'm afraid I'm going to have the same breast cancer that has run in our family for three generations," they are giving the enemy a foothold into their lives.

Recognize what those thoughts and comments are doing. Instead, put your foot down and say, "No more! Today the tide of the battle has turned. That curse has been broken. It stops right here with me."

A *Sound* Mind

For God has not given us a spirit of fear, but of power and of love and of a sound mind.

2 TIMOTHY 1:7 NKJV

MANY PEOPLE DWELL ON THE NEGATIVE and then wonder why nothing positive ever happens to them. It's because their minds are focused in the wrong direction. You can't constantly think thoughts of worry and fear and expect to have any kind of victory in your life. The Scripture tells us God has given us a "sound mind," which the *Amplified Bible* describes as a "well-balanced mind" and adds "discipline and self-control." In other words, we must discipline our minds to think thoughts that are consistent with God's Word.

Every day you will have negative thoughts attack your mind. But you can choose whether or not you will give them life by dwelling on them. You can control the doorway to your mind, reject the negative thoughts, and choose to dwell on what God says.

> This book of the law shall not depart
> from your mouth, but you shall
> meditate on it day and night, so that
> you may be careful to do according to
> all that is written in it; for then you will
> make your way prosperous, and then
> you will have success.
>
> JOSHUA 1:8 NASB

Meditate on God's Word

GOD SAID IF WE'LL think about His Word day and night and fill our minds with thoughts of faith and victory, we will have successful lives. To *meditate* means to think about the same thing over and over. What are you meditating on? What's going on in your mind? Your consistent thoughts will determine what kind of life you live. Although you may not realize it, if you go around full of fear all the time, you are actually believing for the negative. When you do that, don't be surprised if you don't get just what you're believing for.

Overcome Your Fears

I sought the LORD, and he answered me; he delivered me from all my fears.

PSALM 34:4

*I*F FEAR HAS CREATED A STRONGHOLD in your mind, here's an example of how to overcome it. I met a young married woman who had no medical problems but could not conceive a child. She had feared and come to believe that because of her family history, she could not become pregnant.

I said to her, "Expand your horizons and get a fresh vision of what God can do. Look out through eyes of faith and see yourself holding that little baby. Meditate on God's Word. Dwell on the fact that 'the fruit of my womb is blessed' and 'No good thing will God withhold from me when I walk uprightly.' Keep running those thoughts through your heart and mind. Say, 'Father, I thank You that we are well able to conceive this baby.'" Six months later, she became pregnant.

> *But whoever listens to me will live in safety and be at ease, without fear of harm.*
>
> PROVERBS 1:33

Be *Healthy*

*P*ERHAPS YOUR FAMILY is like mine. On my father's side, we have a long history of heart disease. My dad's dad, many of his uncles, and other relatives all died early deaths from heart disease. I could easily believe, *Well, everybody else has had high blood pressure and clogged arteries. I'm going to have the same thing.*

No, I know better than that. I've made up my mind that I'm going to be healthy. I plan to pass down good health and positive attitudes to my children. I'm going to establish a pattern of long life. I don't have to be afraid of getting the same illnesses that somebody else had, not even those to which I may have a predisposition because of my family background or my genes. I choose to act in faith and receive God's blessings and favor.

Perfect Love

> There is no fear in love. But perfect love drives out fear, because fear has to do with punishment. The one who fears is not made perfect in love.
>
> 1 JOHN 4:18

THE THINGS WE FEAR can come upon us. Get in the habit of meditating on God's Word, and you will discover that God has a great plan for your life. You'll find that God is guiding you, that He's bigger than any of your problems, and He can turn any situation around in your favor.

Your thoughts should be, *I know something good is going to happen to me. I know God is at work in my life. I know my business is going to prosper. I know my family is going to thrive; my children are going to excel.* You could see your whole life turn around this morning if you'd simply start thinking thoughts that are consistent with the positive principles of God's Word.

But I am afraid that just as Eve was deceived by the serpent's cunning, your minds may somehow be led astray from your sincere and pure devotion to Christ.

2 CORINTHIANS 11:3

Guard Your Mind

WHEN THE BIBLE SAYS, "Set your minds on things above" (Colossians 3:2), it means that we must continually choose, twenty-four hours a day, to keep our minds on the positive things of God. The apostle Paul provides a great list by which we can evaluate our thoughts: "whatever is pure, whatever is lovely and lovable, whatever is kind and winsome and gracious . . . if there is anything worthy of praise, think on and weigh and take account of these things" (Philippians 4:8 AMP).

You must make a quality choice to keep your mind focused on the good things of God and experience His best for your life. We must be especially on guard during times of adversity, in times of personal challenge.

When *Trouble* Strikes

Strip yourselves of your former nature ...and be constantly renewed in the spirit of your mind [having a fresh mental and spiritual attitude].

EPHESIANS 4:22–23 AMP

*W*HEN TROUBLES STRIKE, often the first thoughts that come to mind are not positive thoughts. Negative thoughts and fear bombard us from every possible angle. If we dwell on the enemy's lies and the negative takes root, it creates an enemy stronghold in our minds from which attacks can be launched. Right there, we must choose to trust God and know that He has great things in store for us.

So how do you ascertain the source of a thought? Easy. If it's a discouraging, destructive thought; if it brings fear, worry, doubt, or unbelief; if the thought makes you feel weak, insecure, or inadequate, it is not from God. Get rid of it immediately. Stay focused and full of hope, knowing that God is fighting your battles for you.

But his delight is in the law of the
LORD, and on his law he meditates
day and night.

PSALM 1:2

Look for
the *Best*

*L*EARN TO LOOK FOR THE BEST in every situation. No matter what you're going through, if you look hard enough and keep the right attitude, you can find something good about the experience. If you get laid off at work, you can choose to be negative. Or, you can say, "God, I know You are in control of my life, and when one door closes, You always open a bigger and better door. So Father, I can't wait to see what You have in store for me."

Psychologists are convinced that our lives move in the direction of our most dominant thoughts. Throughout this day, engage your mind in thoughts of joy, peace, victory, abundance, and blessings, and you will move toward those things, drawing them to yourself at the same time. Now, that's a magnetic personality!

Forward *or* Reverse?

I have chosen the way of truth; I have set my heart on your laws.

PSALM 119:30

OUR MIND IS SIMILAR TO the transmission in a car. We can choose which way we want to go by engaging the gears. It doesn't take any more effort to go forward than it does to go backward. It's all in the decision process. Similarly, we determine by our own choices which way our lives are going to go. If you choose to stay focused on the positive and keep your mind set on the good things of God, all the forces of darkness are not going to be able to keep you from moving forward and fulfilling your destiny. But if you make the mistake of dwelling on the negative, focusing on your problems and your impossibilities, it's similar to putting that car in reverse and backing away from the victory God has in store for you.

You must decide which way you want to go.

For the Kingdom of God is not a matter of what we eat or drink, but of living a life of goodness and peace and joy in the Holy Spirit.

ROMANS 14:17 NLT

Guard *Against* Pessimism

I HEARD A STORY ABOUT TWO FARMERS. When the rain fell, one farmer said, "Thank You, Lord, for watering our crops." But the other farmer said, "Yeah, but if the rain keeps up, it's going to rot the roots." When the sun came out, the positive farmer said, "Thank You, Lord, that our crops are getting the vitamins and minerals they need. We'll have a wonderful harvest this year." But the negative farmer said, "Yeah, but if it keeps up, it's going to scorch those plants. We're never going to make a living."

Don't you know people who are always focused on the negative? Be sure to guard against their negative attitudes infecting your thinking! Stay focused on the positive things in life.

Take Thoughts Captive

We demolish arguments and every pretension that sets itself up against the knowledge of God, and we take captive every thought to make it obedient to Christ.

2 CORINTHIANS 10:5

*I*T IS SO EASY TO SLIP into assuming the worst in life. Perhaps you've been struggling in your marriage, and before long your imagination is running wild, and you've already seen yourself divorced and living single. If you believe it and see it in your imagination long enough, many times those negative things will come to pass.

Always remember: God honors faith; the enemy attacks with fear. When your imagination starts to run, take those thoughts captive, and change what you're seeing. Quit allowing all those negative imaginations to play destructive games with you. This is war! You must take those thoughts captive, and then cast them out of your thinking patterns. If you will dwell on the things of God, He will keep you in perfect peace.

We live by faith, not by sight.

2 CORINTHIANS 5:7

Live by *Faith*

$\mathcal{S}$OME PEOPLE WALK AROUND, and it's almost as though they have a black cloud following them. If they receive a bad report from the doctor, they've practically planned their own funeral by the end of the day. If their business has been a little slow, they are certain they'll be the first one to get laid off. Rather than discipline their thought life and do what the Scripture says, they panic and always find themselves defeated, failing, and struggling.

It is not honoring to God to go around with a nagging, negative feeling, always thinking that something is wrong. You may not even know why you do it, but you tend to think that things are never going to work out well for you. That attitude will keep you from believing for the good things of God. Live in faith, not in fear.

Redirect the Stream

There is a river whose streams make glad the city of God, the holy dwelling places of the Most High.

PSALM 46:4 NASB

*L*ET'S BE REAL. If your thoughts have been running in a negative pattern for month after month, year after year, it's as though they have been eroding a deep riverbed, and the negativity can flow in only one direction. With every pessimistic thought, the riverbed is a bit deeper and the current stronger. It is possible to program your mind into a negative thinking pattern.

Fortunately, we can cause a new river to flow, one going in a positive direction. When you dwell on God's Word and start seeing the best in situations, little by little, one thought at a time, you are redirecting the flow of that river. It may not look like much at first, but as you continue to reject negative thoughts and redirect the flow, you have a new river flowing.

I have set before you life and death, blessing and cursing; therefore choose life, that both you and your descendants may live.

DEUTERONOMY 30:19 NKJV

Transform *Your* Thinking

FRIEND, DON'T SIT BACK and allow negative, critical thoughts to influence your life. The Bible tells to "not conform any longer to the pattern of this world, but be transformed by the renewing of your mind" (Romans 12:2). As you choose faith instead of fear, expecting good things and taking control of your thought life, that negative stream of thoughts will dwindle and a positive river will flow with positive, faith-filled thoughts of victory.

Keep in mind, though, that the river of negativity wasn't formed overnight, nor will it be redirected without some conscious, strenuous effort on your part. God will help you. Stay full of faith. Stay full of joy. Stay full of hope. If you will transform your thinking, God will transform your life.

Rise Up

When you pass through the waters, I will be with you; and when you pass through the rivers, they will not sweep over you. When you walk through the fire, you will not be burned; the flames will not set you ablaze.

ISAIAH 43:2

THIS MORNING, you may be tempted to mull over discouraging thoughts. In the old days, you'd go back to the same old negative river and say, "What in the world am I going to do? God, how am I going to get out of this mess? I guess it's just my lot in life."

But not this time. Now, you can go back to that positive river of faith-filled thoughts of victory. You can rise up and say, "Father, I'm excited about today. Greater is He that is in me than he that is in the world, and I'm coming out of this." Then go out and live your best life now.

So do not fear, for I am with you; do not be dismayed, for I am your God. I will strengthen you and help you; I will uphold you with my righteous right hand.

ISAIAH 41:10

God Is *Not* Limited

DO THESE LIES SOUND FAMILIAR? *You're not smart enough. You were just born into the wrong family. Even your pet dog was always sick!* To believe those kinds of lies will set limits in your life that will be nearly impossible to rise above.

Here's the truth: God is not limited by your family tree. He is not limited by your education, your social standing, your economic status, or your race. There is no such thing as the wrong side of the tracks with our God. If you will put your trust in Him, God will make your life significant. God longs to make something great out of your life. No, the only thing that limits God is your lack of faith.

A *Can-Do* Mentality

How precious to me are your thoughts, O God! How vast is the sum of them!

PSALM 139:17

THE ENEMY ATTACKS YOUR mind saying that you don't have what it takes; God says you do have what it takes. The enemy says you're not able to succeed; God says you can do all things through Christ. The enemy says you're never going to get well; God says He will restore your health. The enemy says your problems are too big, there's no hope; God says He will solve those problems. Not only that, but He will turn those problems around and use them for your good. Whom are you going to believe?

Friend, God's thoughts will fill you with faith, hope, and victory. God's thoughts will build you up and encourage you. They will give you the strength you need to keep on keeping on. God's thoughts will give you that can-do mentality.

*Now to him who is able to do
immeasurably more than all we ask
or imagine, according to his power that
is at work within us...*

EPHESIANS 3:20

Immeasurably More

A LITTLE BOY WENT OUT TO the backyard to play with a baseball bat and ball. He said to himself, "I am the best hitter in the world." Then he threw the ball up in the air and took a swing at it, but missed. Without a moment's hesitation, he tossed it in the air again, saying as he swung the bat, "I'm the best hitter in the world," but missed. Strike two. He tossed the ball up again, even more determined, saying, "I am the best hitter in the world!" But he missed again. Strike three. The boy laid down his bat and smiled real big. "What do you know?" he said. "I'm the best pitcher in the world!"

If things don't work out as planned today, look for something good in your circumstances. Fill your mind with good thoughts.

Escape the Corruption

Through these he has given us his very great and precious promises, so that through them you may participate in the divine nature and escape the corruption in the world caused by evil desires.

2 PETER 1:4

*Y*OU CAN HAVE THE MOST POWERFUL computer in the world, but if one of the myriad of computer viruses lurking in cyberspace is allowed to get in and contaminate the software, it can destroy your hard drive and the information stored in your computer. All too often, you unwittingly pass along the virus to others, exacerbating the problem.

Similarly, if we allow negative thoughts and deceptions to access our minds, they will subtly corrupt our minds, attitudes, and values. Created in the image of God to be happy, healthy, and whole, our thinking becomes contaminated with worries and feelings of inadequacy and insecurity. Making matters worse, we pass these negative attitudes to others. Our only safeguard is to keep our thoughts aligned with God's Word.

Incline your ear and hear the words of the wise, and apply your mind to my knowledge; for it will be pleasant if you keep them within you, that they may be ready on your lips. So that your trust may be in the LORD.

PROVERBS 22:17–19 NASB

Reprogram Your Computer

WHEN YOU RECOGNIZE THAT you've allowed negative thoughts to be copied onto your mental "hard drive," you must reprogram your mind by changing your thinking. If you keep your mind focused on the good things of God, the Bible says that God will keep you in perfect peace in the midst of your storms (see Isaiah 26:3).

Dwell on the fact that Almighty God is on your side. Stand on the fact that He's promised to fight your battles for you. Dwell on the truth that no weapon formed against you can prosper. If you start thinking these kinds of thoughts, you will be filled with faith and confidence, no matter what comes against you today.

Be a *Victor*

> But thanks be to God!
> He gives us the victory through
> our Lord Jesus Christ.
>
> 1 CORINTHIANS 15:57

TO LIVE YOUR BEST LIFE NOW requires that you believe you are a victor and not a victim. When you go through disappointments in life—and we all do—or when you face a setback and it looks as though one of your dreams has died, keep believing. When it looks dark and dreary and you don't see any way out, remind yourself that your heavenly Father created the whole universe. He is in control of your life, guiding and directing your steps. His plans for you are good and not evil. Don't make the mistake of sitting around feeling sorry for yourself. No, put on a fresh new attitude. Take what God has given you and make the most of it.

You know the truth; it's time to allow that truth to set you free.

Then Caleb quieted the people
before Moses, and said, "Let us go
up at once and take possession, for
we are well able to overcome it."

NUMBERS 13:30 NKJV

Possess the Land

THIS MORNING, recall how the children of Israel had been miraculously delivered from the Egyptians and were camped right next door to the Promised Land, but didn't go in for fear of giants. Don't allow a similar lack of faith or a wrong mind-set to rob you of your destiny. Maybe you are camped right next door to your Promised Land. God has great things He wants to do in your life. He wants to increase you, heal your body, restore your marriage, or bless you financially. Maybe you are right on the edge of a miracle!

If you will get your thinking lined up with God's thinking, nothing will be able to stop you. No obstacle will be too high, no situation too difficult. If you believe God's Word, all things are possible.

Keep Pressing Forward

Hear, O Israel, today you are going into battle against your enemies. Do not be fainthearted or afraid; do not be terrified or give way to panic before them. For the LORD your God is the one who goes with you to fight for you against your enemies to give you victory.

DEUTERONOMY 20:3–4

REMEMBER, THE ENEMY always fights the hardest when he knows God has something great in store for you. The darkest battle, the darkest storm, will always give way to the brightest sunrise. Keep believing, keep praying, keep pressing forward. The Scripture says, "Don't get tired of doing what's right, for in due season you shall reap if you faint not" (see Galatians 6:9). It may be hard right now, but remind yourself that you have the power of God inside you.

God said you are well able to fulfill your destiny. You can do what you need to do.

> The LORD is my light and my
> salvation—whom shall I fear?
> The LORD is the stronghold of my
> life—of whom shall I be afraid?
>
> PSALM 27:1

Go with God

WHEN MY FATHER died back in 1999, I knew deep inside that I was to pastor Lakewood Church, but all I could see were the gigantic reasons why I couldn't do it. I thought, *God, I don't feel qualified. I have only preached once. I've never been to seminary.* I had to decide whether I was going to shrink back into my comfort zone or step out in faith, knowing that Almighty God was on my side.

I decided to go with God, but it wasn't easy. Several Sunday mornings I got up and thought, *I can't do this!* But I'd go stand before the mirror, look myself right in the eyes, and say, "Joel, you can do it in the power of His might." I did it, and you can as well.

Be Consistent

When a man's ways are pleasing to the LORD, he makes even his enemies to be at peace with him.

PROVERBS 16:7 NASB

SOME PEOPLE TAKE one step forward in faith and then two steps backward. They are happy and in a good attitude one day, then the next day they are negative and depressed. They make a little progress, then they back up. Because of their vacillating faith, they never really get to the place God wants them to be. They never experience the victories He has in store for them.

Friend, you must be consistent. Your attitude should be: *I refuse to go backward. I am going forward with God. I'm going to be the person He wants me to be. I'm going to fulfill my destiny.* If you will maintain that mind-set, God will continually work in your life. If you will trust in God, He'll fight your battles for you.

"Have faith in God," Jesus answered.

MARK 11:22

Stand Strong

I T DOESN'T MATTER WHAT you're going through, or how big your opponents are. Keep an attitude of faith. Stay calm. Stay in a positive frame of mind. And don't try to do it all your own way. Let God do it His way. If you will simply obey His commands, He will change things in your favor.

The Bible says, "Don't get weary and faint in your mind" (see Hebrews 12:3). Remember, stand strong. When negative thoughts come, reject them and replace them with God's thoughts. When you're in that attitude of faith, you are opening the door for God to work in your situation. You may not see anything happening with your natural eyes, but in the unseen realm, in the spiritual world, God is at work. And if you'll do your part and keep believing, at the right time, God will bring you out with the victory.

You Get What *You* Say

May the words of my mouth and the meditation of my heart be pleasing in your sight, O LORD, my Rock and my Redeemer.

PSALM 19:14

*I*N THE LATE 1990s, Jose Lima starred as a pitcher for the Houston Astros. Jose is an outgoing, energetic, likable young ballplayer who usually exudes a positive attitude. But when the Astros moved into their new ballpark, which has one of the shortest distances from home plate to the left-field fence of any ballpark in Major League Baseball, he walked out to the pitcher's mound and said, "I'll never be able to pitch in here." That season, Jose had the worst year of his career. He went from being a twenty-game winner to being a sixteen-game loser in back-to-back seasons.

What happened? The same thing that happens to many of us every day—we get what we say. Our words become self-fulfilling prophecies. Negative thoughts give birth to negative words, and negative actions follow.

Death and life are in the power
of the tongue, and those who love
it will eat its fruit.

PROVERBS 18:21 NASB

The Power of *Your* Words

OUR WORDS have tremendous power and are similar to seeds. By speaking them aloud, they are planted in our subconscious minds, take root, grow, and produce fruit of the same kind. Whether we speak positive or negative words, we will reap exactly what we sow. That's why we need to be extremely careful what we think and say.

The Bible compares the tongue to the small rudder of a huge ship, which controls the ship's direction (see James 3:4). Similarly, your tongue will control the direction of your life. You create an environment for either good or evil with your words, and if you're always murmuring, complaining, and talking about how bad life is treating you, you're going to live in a pretty miserable world. Use your words to *change* your negative situations and fill them with life.

Say It Boldly

So we say with confidence, "The Lord is my helper; I will not be afraid. What can man do to me?"

HEBREWS 13:6

I HEARD ABOUT A DOCTOR who understood the power of words. One prescription he gave to all his patients was for them to say at least once every hour, "I'm getting better and better every day, in every way." His patients experienced amazing results, much better than the patients treated by many of his colleagues.

When you say something often enough, with enthusiasm and passion, before long your subconscious mind begins to act on what you are saying, doing whatever is necessary to bring those thoughts and words to pass. If you struggle with low self-esteem, go overboard in speaking words of victory about your life. Get up each morning and say, "I am valuable and loved. God has a great plan for my life. I'm excited about my future." There truly is power in your words.

Speak to Your Mountains

Truly I say to you, whoever says to this mountain, "Be taken up and cast into the sea," and does not doubt in his heart, but believes that what he says is going to happen, it will be granted him. Therefore I say to you, all things for which you pray and ask, believe that you have received them, and they will be granted you.

MARK 11:23–24 NASB

*W*HAT MOUNTAIN IS IN FRONT of you this morning—a sickness, a troubled relationship, a floundering business? Jesus said that whatever your mountain is, you must do more than think or pray about it; you must speak to that obstacle.

The Bible says, "Let the weakling say, 'I am strong'" (Joel 3:10). Start calling yourself healed, happy, whole, blessed, and prosperous. God is a miracle-working God. Stop talking to God about how big your mountains are, and start talking to your mountains about how big your God is!

In the
Name of
the Lord

I have strength for all things in Christ Who empowers me.

PHILIPPIANS 4:13 AMP

WHEN DAVID FACED the giant Goliath, he didn't complain and say, "God, why do I always have huge problems?" He didn't dwell on the fact that Goliath was three times his size or that Goliath was a skilled warrior and he was just a shepherd boy. Rather than focus on the magnitude of the obstacle before him, David chose to focus on the greatness of God.

David looked Goliath right in the eyes and spoke aloud these words of faith: "You come against me with sword and spear and javelin, but I come against you in the name of the LORD Almighty, the God of the armies of Israel, whom you have defied" (1 Samuel 17:45). He didn't merely *think* them; he didn't simply *pray* them, but he spoke directly to the mountain of a man and brought him down.

> *For it is with your heart that you believe and are justified, and it is with your mouth that you confess and are saved. As the Scripture says, "Anyone who trusts in him will never be put to shame."*
>
> ROMANS 10:10–11

The *Miracle* in Your Mouth

FRIEND, there is a miracle in your mouth. If you want to change your world, start by changing your words. When you're facing obstacles in your path, you must boldly say, "Greater is He who is in me than he who is in the world" (see 1 John 4:4); "No weapon formed against me is going to prosper" (see Isaiah 54:17); and "God always causes me to triumph."

Quit complaining about poverty or lack and start declaring, "God supplies all of my needs in abundance." Quit complaining that nothing good ever happens to you and start declaring, "Everything I touch prospers and succeeds." Stop cursing the darkness, and use your words to command light to come into your situation. Your words have that power.

Healing Words

My son, give attention to my words; incline your ear to my sayings. Do not let them depart from your eyes; keep them in the midst of your heart; for they are life to those who find them, and health to all their flesh.

PROVERBS 4:20–22 NKJV

*I*N 1981, MY MOTHER was diagnosed with cancer and given a few weeks to live. But my mother refused to complain about how sick or weak she felt or how hopeless her situation looked. No, she wrote down about forty favorite passages of Scripture concerning healing, and all day she'd read over them and boldly declare, "With long life, He satisfies me and shows me His salvation." Slowly, week after week, she began to feel better. She kept on confessing God's Word, and more than twenty years later, she remains cancer-free, healed by the power of God and His Word!

My mother used her words to change her world, and you can do the same thing.

But the word is very near you, in your mouth and in your heart, that you may observe it.

DEUTERONOMY 30:14 NASB

Speak Words of *Faith*

WHEN IT COMES TO OUR WORDS, many times we are our own worst enemies. We may blame everybody and everything else, but the truth is, we are profoundly influenced by what we say about ourselves. Scripture says, "You are snared by the words of your mouth; you are taken by the words of your mouth" (Proverbs 6:2 NKJV).

Our words are vital in bringing our dreams to pass. It's not enough to simply see it by faith or in your imagination. You have to begin speaking words of faith, victory, health, and success over your life. Your words have enormous creative power. The moment you speak something out, you give birth to it. This is a spiritual principle, and it works whether what you are saying is positive or negative, so make them words of faith.

Boldly *Confess* God's Word

Reckless words pierce like a sword, but the tongue of the wise brings healing.

PROVERBS 12:18

IF NEGATIVE STATEMENTS such as "Nothing good ever happens to me" are the norm in your life, they will literally prevent you from moving ahead in life. That's why you must learn to guard your tongue and speak only faith-filled words over your life. This is one of the most important principles you can ever grab hold of. Simply put, your words can make or break you.

Understand, avoiding negative talk is not enough. You must start using your words to move forward in life. When you believe God's Word and begin to boldly confess it, mixing it with your faith, you are actually confirming that truth and making it valid in your own life. And all heaven comes to attention to back up God's Word, bringing to life the great things God has in store for you.

My tongue will speak of your righteousness and of your praises all day long.

PSALM 35:28

Speak of His *Goodness*

GOD NEVER COMMANDED us to repeatedly verbalize our pain and suffering. He didn't instruct us to go around discussing our negative situations with our friends and neighbors. Instead, God told us to speak constantly of His goodness, to speak of His promises in the morning at the breakfast table, in the evenings around the dinner table, at night before bedtime, continually dwelling on the good things of God.

You could experience a new sense of joy in your home, if you'd simply stop talking about the negative things in your life and begin talking about God's Word. If you are always talking about your problems, don't be surprised if you live in perpetual defeat. Quit speaking words of defeat, and start speaking words of victory. Don't use your words to describe your situation; use your words to change your situation.

Get on the *Offense*

Finally, be strong in the Lord and in his mighty power.

EPHESIANS 6:10

*M*AYBE YOU ARE FACING A "hopeless" situation. Don't give up. God is a miracle-working God. He knows what you're going through, and He will not let you down.

While you need a strong defense, you also need to get on the offense. You have to be aggressive. Set a powerful tone for the entire day as soon as you get out of bed. If you wait until you have read the morning newspaper, you'll start your day with all sorts of sad, dreary news. Try starting your day with some good news by speaking God's Word over your life! The moment you wake up, begin to give new life to your dreams by speaking words of victory. Start speaking words of faith today, and watch how God causes your circumstances to change.

You are my hiding place; you will protect me from trouble and surround me with songs of deliverance.

PSALM 32:7

Songs of Deliverance

GOD HAS NOT GIVEN US hundreds of promises in His Word simply for us to read and enjoy. God has given us His promises so we might boldly declare them to bring us victory, health, hope, and abundant life. The Scripture says, "With the heart one believes unto righteousness, and with the mouth confession is made unto salvation" (Romans 10:10 NKJV). When you believe God's Word and begin to speak it, mixing it with faith, you are actually confirming that truth and making it valid in your own life.

If you are facing sickness or struggling financially today, boldly declare what the Word of God has to say about it. Friend, when you make those kinds of bold declarations, God will work to accomplish all that His Word says.

The
Power of
Blessing

Out of the same mouth proceed blessing and cursing. My brethren, these things ought not to be so.

JAMES 3:10 NKJV

WHETHER WE REALIZE IT or not, our words affect our children's future for either good or evil. If you want your son or daughter to be productive and successful, you need to begin declaring words of life over your children rather than predictions of doom and despair. We need to speak loving words of approval and acceptance, words that encourage, inspire, and motivate our family members and friends to reach for new heights. We are speaking abundance and increase, declaring God's favor in their lives.

Use your words to speak blessing over people. Husbands, bless your wives with your words. You can help set the direction for your employees with your positive words. Learn to speak blessings over your friends. Start speaking those blessings today!

> *All these are the twelve tribes of Israel, and this is what their father said to them when he blessed them, giving each the blessing appropriate to him.*
>
> GENESIS 49:28

Speak *Loving* Words

*I*N THE OLD TESTAMENT, the people clearly understood the power of the blessing. As the family patriarch approached senility or death, the father would lay his hands on each of his sons' heads and speak loving, faith-filled words over them about their future, which constituted "the blessing." Many times, children even fought over the father's blessing. They weren't fighting over money or the family business they might inherit. No, the family realized that these faith-filled words carried spiritual authority and had the ability to bring success, prosperity, and health into their future. Beyond that, they deeply desired the blessing from someone they loved and respected.

The words we speak to our children can carry the same spiritual authority with all the power of blessing to them.

Words That *Impact* Forever

May God give you of heaven's dew and of earth's richness—an abundance of grain and new wine.

GENESIS 27:28

ONE OF THE MOST AMAZING biblical records concerning the power of the blessing comes out of the lives of Jacob and Esau, the two sons of Isaac (see Genesis 27:1–41). Jacob wanted his father's blessing—not just any blessing, but the blessing that rightfully belonged to Esau, the firstborn son in the family. Isaac was old, near death, and practically blind. One day, Jacob's mother, Rebekah, took advantage of a situation in the home and directed Jacob to deceive his father and get the blessing for himself. Jacob understood that he was risking his entire future on this gambit. He recognized that the words his father spoke over him would impact him, for either good or evil, the rest of his life.

Realize that your words will impact your children long after they are grown and have children of their own.

A word aptly spoken is like apples of gold in settings of silver.

PROVERBS 25:11

Speak a Blessing Today

*N*EGATIVE WORDS CAN DESTROY a person. You cannot speak negatively about someone on one hand, then turn around and expect that person to be blessed. In that regard, we are often too harsh and fault-finding with our children and loved ones. Our negative words can cause them to lose the sense of value God has placed within them and can allow the enemy to bring all kinds of insecurity and inferiority into their lives.

What are you passing down to the next generation? It's not enough to think it; you must vocalize it. A blessing is not a blessing until it is spoken. Your children need to hear you say words such as, "I love you. I believe in you. I think you're great. There's nobody else like you." They need to hear your approval. They need to feel your love. They need your blessing. Say it today!

Bless the Children

The LORD gave me this message: "I knew you before I formed you in your mother's womb. Before you were born I set you apart and appointed you as my prophet to the nations."

JEREMIAH 1:4–5 NLT

*A*S PARENTS, we have a responsibility before God and society to train our precious children, to discipline them when they disobey, to lovingly correct them when they make wrong choices. But we should not constantly harp on our kids. If you continually speak words that discourage and dishearten, before long you will destroy your child's self-image. Millions of adults today are still suffering as a result of the negative words their parents spoke over them as children.

What words do you use with your children? God will hold you responsible for your words and their impact. With authority comes responsibility, and you have the responsibility as the spiritual authority over your child to make sure that he feels loved, accepted, and approved.

Fathers, do not exasperate your children; instead, bring them up in the training and instruction of the Lord.

EPHESIANS 6:4

Be *Careful* with Your Words

MOST PARENTS WANT THE best for their children, and there are many situations where a parent must confront and correct them. But even a well-meaning parent can speak the kind of negative words that will destroy a person quicker than you can imagine. "Why can't you make better grades?" "You didn't mow the lawn right." "Go clean your room—it looks like a pigpen!" "You can't do anything right, can you?"

Do you see the power of your words? Be extremely careful about what you allow to come out of your mouth. The next time you're tempted to talk down to somebody, to belittle your child or degrade him, remember, you can't ever get those words back. Once you speak them, they take on a life of their own. Make sure it's a good life.

Model God's *Character*

As a father has compassion on his children, so the LORD has compassion on those who fear him.

PSALM 103:13

NOBODY COULD HAVE REPRESENTED the goodness of God any better to us Osteen kids than my dad did. Even when we made mistakes or got off track, while Daddy was firm, he was also loving and kind. He nurtured us back to the right course. He never beat us into line; he loved us onto the right path. Although he was very busy, he always took time for us. He encouraged us to do great things, to fulfill our dreams.

If you are a father, you need to realize that most children get their concepts of who God is and what He is like from their fathers. If the father is mean, critical, and harsh, inevitably the children will grow up with a distorted view of God. If the father is loving, kind, compassionate, and just, the children will better understand God's character.

The LORD bless you and keep you; the LORD make his face shine upon you and be gracious to you.

NUMBERS 6:24–25

Declare God's *Goodness*

MY SIBLINGS AND I were not perfect kids. But my parents never focused on our weaknesses or on the problems. They always focused on the solutions. They constantly told us we were the best kids in the world. And we grew up secure, knowing not only that our parents loved each other, but they also loved us and believed the best in us. They were going to stand behind us through thick and thin.

If you want to bless your children, start declaring God's goodness in their lives. Start boldly declaring, "God's face is smiling toward you, and He longs to be good to you. I declare that you are blessed with an obedient heart, with success, with supernatural wisdom, and you have clear direction for your life."

Generation to *Generation*

His descendants will be mighty on earth; the generation of the upright will be blessed.

PSALM 112:2 NKJV

$\mathcal{B}$ECAUSE I GREW UP WITH acceptance and approval from my parents, now, as a father myself, I'm speaking words of blessing into my children's lives that will be passed down to another generation, and on and on. Before our children go to bed, Victoria and I tell them, "There's nothing you can't do. You have a bright future in front of you. You're surrounded by God's favor. Everything you touch is going to prosper." We believe we have an opportunity and a responsibility to speak God's blessings into our children now, while they are young.

Don't wait until your children are teenagers or in their twenties and about to get married to begin praying for God's blessings in their lives. No, declare God's blessings over them all the days of their lives, starting this morning.

> *Let each one of you in particular so love his own wife as himself, and let the wife see that she respects her husband.*
>
> EPHESIANS 5:33 NKJV

Wonder in a *Marriage*

*I*T IS IMPORTANT FOR A HUSBAND TO understand that his words have tremendous power in his wife's life. One of the leading causes of emotional breakdowns among married women is the fact that women do not feel valued. One of the main reasons for that deficiency is because husbands are willfully or unwittingly withholding the words of approval women so desperately desire.

If you want to see God do wonders in your marriage, start praising your spouse. Start appreciating and encouraging her. Every single day, a husband should tell his wife, "I love you. I appreciate you. You're the best thing that ever happened to me." A wife should do the same for her husband. Your relationship would improve immensely if you'd simply start speaking kind, positive words that bless your spouse.

Let Go of the *Past*

I—yes, I alone—will blot out your sins for my own sake and will never think of them again.

ISAIAH 43:25 NLT

EVERYBODY GOES THROUGH disappointments and setbacks from time to time, but if we hold on to hurt and pain, we end up living negative and bitter lives. Maybe you've made some mistakes or some poor choices, and now you're tempted to sit around feeling guilty and condemned, thinking you wish you had chosen another career or married that other person.

It's so easy to live life focused on that rearview mirror. We can't do anything about the past, and we have no guarantees regarding the future; we can only do something about right now. The good news is, your past does not have to poison your future. God still has good things in store for you. He wants to take that negative situation, turn it around, and use it to your advantage.

Come to me, all you who are weary and burdened, and I will give you rest. Take my yoke upon you and learn from me, for I am gentle and humble in heart, and you will find rest for your souls.

MATTHEW 11:28–29

Life Isn't Fair

WE LIVE IN A SOCIETY that loves to make excuses, and one of our favorite phrases is: "It's not my fault." But the truth is, if we are bitter and resentful, it's because we are allowing ourselves to remain that way. We've all had negative things happen to us. If you look hard enough, anyone can make excuses and blame the past for his bad attitude, poor choices, or hot temper.

It's time to let go of your excuses and to get rid of your victim mentality. Nobody—not even God—ever promised that life would be fair. If you bring it all to Jesus and let it go, today can be a new beginning.

New Mercies

Through the LORD's mercies we are not consumed, because His compassions fail not. They are new every morning; great is Your faithfulness.

LAMENTATIONS 3:22–23 NKJV

WHEN YOU GET UP EACH MORNING, one of the first things you should do is shake off the disappointments of yesterday. Discard discouragement, guilt, and condemnation. Your attitude should be, *It's a new day, and I'm not going to drag the hurts of yesterday into this day. I'm going to start afresh.*

God's mercies are new every morning. You may have made a lot of mistakes, but God has not run out of mercy. He makes a fresh new batch every single morning. Do you know why? Because He knew we were going to use up all that He made yesterday! You may have done something last week that you're not proud of, but you don't have to carry that around with you any longer. You simply need to receive God's mercy and forgiveness.

And when you stand praying, if you hold anything against anyone, forgive him, so that your Father in heaven may forgive you your sins.

MARK 11:25

Quit Comparing

YOU MAY HAVE VALID reasons for feeling sorry for yourself. You may have gone through things that nobody deserves to experience in life—physical, verbal, sexual, or emotional abuse. Maybe you've struggled with a chronic illness or an irreparable physical problem. Maybe your dreams didn't work out. I don't mean to minimize those difficult experiences, but if you want to live in victory, you can't let your past poison your future.

It's time to allow your emotional wounds to heal. Quit comparing your life to someone else's, and quit dwelling on what could or should have been. Quit asking questions such as, "Why this?" or "Why that?" or "Why me?" Let go of those hurts and pains. Forgive the people who did you wrong. Forgive yourself for the mistakes you've made.

Shake Off the Baggage

You will know the truth, and the truth will set you free.

JOHN 8:32

RIEND, don't be a prisoner of the past. Some people are always dwelling on their disappointments. They can't understand why their prayers aren't being answered, why their loved one wasn't healed, why they were mistreated. Some people have lived so long in self-pity that it has become part of their identity. They don't realize that God wants to restore what's been stolen.

If you're not willing to let go of the old, don't expect God to do the new. If you've had some unfair things happen to you, make a decision that you're going to quit reliving those things in your memory. Instead, think on good things, things that will build you up and not tear you down, things that will encourage you and give you the hope that there's a brighter tomorrow.

You'll use the old rubble of past lives to build anew, rebuild the foundations from out of your past. You'll be known as those who can fix anything, restore old ruins, rebuild and renovate, make the community livable again.

ISAIAH 58:12 THE MESSAGE

Move Forward

*I*F YOU'RE GOING TO go forward in life, you must quit looking backward. Why? Because your life is going to follow your thoughts. If you're constantly dwelling on all the negative things that have happened to you, focused on what you've done wrong, you're perpetuating that problem. You will never be truly happy as long as you harbor bitterness in your heart.

Perhaps you've been blaming God for taking one of your loved ones or because your situation didn't work out after you prayed about it. If you don't deal with it, you will wallow in self-pity. You must let go of those negative attitudes and the accompanying anger. Let it go.

Change the *Channel*

> Those who live in accordance with the Spirit have their minds set on what the Spirit desires.
>
> ROMANS 8:5

*I*F WE SEE SOMETHING WE don't like on TV, we just flip channels with the remote control. We need to learn how to mentally change channels when negative images of the past pop up in our minds unexpectedly. Unfortunately, when some people see those negative experiences on their minds' "screens," instead of quickly changing channels, they pull up a chair and get some popcorn, as though they're going to watch a good movie. They willingly allow themselves to relive all those hurts and pains. And then they wonder why they are depressed, upset, or discouraged.

Learn to change the channel. Don't let your mind or your emotions drag you down into despair. Instead, dwell on the good things God has done in your life.

Jesus replied, "No one who puts his hand to the plow and looks back is fit for service in the kingdom of God."

Don't Go There

WHEN WE KEEP reliving the painful memories of the past, we negate God's desire to bring healing. Just as we are about to heal, we start talking about it, seeing it in our imagination. All of a sudden, we can feel those same emotions all over again, tearing open the old wound. It will never properly heal until we learn to leave it alone. When you dwell on painful experiences in your past, your emotions go right back there with you, and you feel the pain as vividly in the present as when it happened twenty years ago.

Refuse to go back there emotionally; refuse to dredge up negative emotional memories. Recounting painful experiences will do you no good; in fact, strongly felt negative emotions hold the potential to severely stifle your progress.

Dealing with a Loss

Now when the days of his mourning were past, Joseph spoke...

GENESIS 50:4 NKJV

THIS MORNING, perhaps you're still dealing with the loss of a loved one. After my father died, I remember being all alone in my parents' house and walking through the den where he had his heart attack. In my imagination, I could see it all happening again, and I began to feel those same emotions of despair, sadness, and discouragement from that night. Right then, I made a decision to not allow myself to relive that night. Rather than dwelling on the hurt from the past, I purposely started recalling all the good times that my dad and I had known in that den. In my mind, I could see Daddy playing with our children. I recalled his great sense of humor.

Notice, it didn't happen naturally; it was a decision I had to make, and you will, too.

Within your temple, O God, we meditate on your unfailing love.

PSALM 48:9

Throw Away the *Key*

EVERY PERSON HAS TWO MAIN FILES in his or her memory system. The first file is filled with all the good things that have happened to us—our victories and accomplishments, the things that have brought us joy and happiness. The second file is filled with all the negative things—our hurts and pains, defeats and failures, things that brought us sadness and sorrow. Throughout life, we can choose which file we access. Some people repeatedly return to file number two and relive the painful things that have happened to them. They practically wear out file number two, and they never get around to exploring file number one.

If you want to be free, if you want to overcome self-pity, throw away the key to file number two. Keep your mind focused on the good things God has done in your life.

Drop the *Baggage*

My guilt has overwhelmed me like a burden too heavy to bear.

PSALM 38:4

*M*ANY PEOPLE WONDER WHY they're not happy. Often, it's because they are dragging around all sorts of baggage from the past. Somebody offended them last week, so they have packed that pain in their bag. They lost their temper, said some things they shouldn't have, and they have that stuffed in their bag, too. Growing up, they weren't treated right. They've got that suitcase full of junk, too. Worse yet, they drag their baggage with them everywhere they go. Not only do they hold on to their baggage, but they like to unpack it every once in a while, just to make sure it's all still there. They've been carrying these heavy bags for years; they are loaded down by their collection of burdens.

This morning, drop any emotional baggage you're dragging and step toward a rich, full life!

*Each heart knows its own bitterness,
and no one else can share its joy.*

PROVERBS 14:10

Lay It Aside

MARIE (not her real name) went through a failed relationship in her marriage many years ago. She prayed that God would bring somebody new into her life. Sure enough, she met a fine gentleman, a very godly, successful man, and she was excited about their friendship. But when they were together, all she talked about was how terrible her marriage had been. Finally, he stopped calling her and just moved on.

If you hold on to the hurts and pains of the past, they will poison you wherever you go and keep you from experiencing good, healthy relationships. You may think that other people are the problem, but examine your own heart. Quit mourning over something that's over and done. God says that you need to lay it aside and get rid of whatever entangles you (see Hebrews 12:1).

Good Things in Store

You have made known to me the path of life; you will fill me with joy in your presence, with eternal pleasures at your right hand.

PSALM 16:11

FRIEND, GOD IS BIGGER than your past, your disappointments, and your problems. You may have made a lot of mistakes, but God can turn those things all around. People may have hurt you and done you wrong, but if you'll leave it up to God, He'll pay you back. He'll make your wrongs right. Start focusing on your possibilities. Let hope fill your heart.

No matter what you've been through, God is saying there are great days ahead for you. Say, "I'm not going to be a prisoner of my past. I've had enough. I'm going to stop focusing on my disappointments. I'm moving on with my life, knowing that God has good things in store." If you'll develop that kind of attitude, God will give you a new beginning.

When Jesus noticed him lying there [helpless], knowing that he had already been a long time in that condition, He said to him, "Do you want to become well? [Are you really in earnest about getting well?]

JOHN 5:6 AMP

Get Up and Get *Movin'*

A MAN IN JERUSALEM HAD been crippled for thirty-eight years. He spent every day of his life lying by the pool of Bethesda, hoping for a miracle (see John 5). When Jesus saw the man lying there, He asked a simple, straightforward question: "Do you want to be made well?" The man's response was interesting. He began listing all of his excuses. "I'm all alone. I don't have anyone to help me." Is it any wonder that he had not been healed?

Jesus looked at him and said, in effect, "If you are serious about getting well, if you want to get out of this mess, get up off the ground, take up your bed, and be on your way." When the man did what Jesus told him to do, he was miraculously healed!

Step into *Your* Future

Let us also lay aside every encumbrance and the sin which so easily entangles us, and let us run with endurance the race that is set before us.

HEBREWS 12:1 NASB

IN JOHN 5, the crippled man had a deep-seated, lingering disorder similar to what many people have today. Their maladies may be emotional instead of physical, but they are deep-seated, lingering disorders nonetheless. They may stem from unforgiveness or holding on to past resentments, and they affect their personality, their relationships, and their self-image. Just as the man lying by the pool, some people sit back for years, waiting for a miracle to happen that will make everything better.

If you're serious about being well, you can't lie around feeling sorry for yourself. Stop making excuses. Today can be a turning point in your life. Trust God, get up, and step into the great future He has for you.

I do believe, but help me overcome my unbelief!

MARK 9:24 NLT

Do You *Want* to Be Well?

*Y*OU DO NOT HAVE TO live depressed and discouraged, if you refuse to live with a victim mentality. You might be saying, "I just don't understand why this is happening to me. I don't understand why I got sick. Why did my loved one die? Why did my marriage break apart? Why was I raised in such an abusive environment?" But don't use that as an excuse to wallow in self-pity, because you will sink deeper and deeper.

This morning can be a turning point in your life, a season of new beginnings. Muster enough faith to say, "God, I don't understand it, but I trust You to make something good out of it. You're a good God, and I know You have my best interests at heart. You promised that all things will work together for my good." That is faith, and that is the attitude God honors.

Reach for New *Heights*

*And she was in bitterness of soul, and prayed to the L*ORD *and wept in anguish.*

1 SAMUEL 1:10 NKJV

WHEN MY MOTHER WAS growing up, she developed the dreaded disease of polio. She had to wear a heavy brace on her leg for many years, and even today, one leg remains shorter than the other. Mother could have easily said, "God, why did this happen to me?" But she refused to see herself as the victim, and God brought her out of that difficulty.

Difficulties can make you bitter, or they can make you better. They can drag you down and make you a sour person, or they can inspire you to reach for new heights. It's easy to make excuses, have a bad attitude, or have a poor self-image. Anyone can do that. But if you want to live your best life now, you must reach out to God, shake off self-pity, get up, and move on with your life.

Do not judge, and you will not be judged. Do not condemn, and you will not be condemned. Forgive, and you will be forgiven.

LUKE 6:37

Don't Become Bitter

KING DAVID PRAYED AND FASTED FOR seven days, nevertheless his newborn baby died (see 2 Samuel 12:1–25). Although David had been extremely distraught, he did not get bitter or question God. Instead, he dared to trust God in the midst of his disappointment. He washed his face and moved on with his life.

When you go through situations you don't understand, don't become bitter. Learn to do what David did: just wash your face, keep a good attitude, and move on. If you will stay in an attitude of faith and victory, God has promised that He will turn those emotional wounds around. He'll use them to your advantage, and you will come out better than you would have had they not happened to you.

The "Why" Questions

Far be it from you! Will not the Judge of all the earth do right?

GENESIS 18:25

DON'T WASTE ANOTHER MINUTE trying to figure out why certain evil things have happened to you or your loved ones. You may never know the answer. But don't use that as an excuse to wallow in self-pity. Leave it alone and move on with your life. Trust God and accept the fact that there will be some unanswered questions. Just because you don't know the answer doesn't mean one does not exist.

Each of us should have what I call an "I Don't Understand It" file. When something comes up for which you have no reasonable answer, instead of dwelling on the "why," simply place it in this file and walk away from any emotional bondage in which you have been living.

> *Make every effort to live in peace with all men and to be holy; without holiness no one will see the Lord. See to it that no one misses the grace of God and that no bitter root grows up to cause trouble and defile many.*
>
> HEBREWS 12:14–15

Get to the *Root*

A LOT OF PEOPLE are trying to improve their lives by dealing with the external aspects. They are attempting to rectify their bad habits, bad attitudes, bad tempers, or negative and sour personalities. Trying to change the fruit of their lives is noble, but unless they get to the root, they will never change the fruit. As long as a bitter internal root is growing, the problems will persist. You may be able to control your behavior or keep a good attitude for a while, but you can't be free.

You have to go deeper and get to the root to be able to deal with the problem, overcome it, and truly begin to change.

The Power of *Forgiveness*

Forgive us our sins, as we have forgiven those who sin against us.

MATTHEW 6:12 NLT

*I*F YOU HAVE AREAS IN your life where you are constantly struggling, trying to change but finding yourself unable to do so, ask God to show you what's keeping you from being free.

A young woman once came to my dad for spiritual help. She had been sexually assaulted by several boys when she was in her teens. Consequently, she could not have an intimate relationship with her husband. She realized that all that anger and hatred in her heart was affecting her relationship with her husband. She knew it wasn't going to be easy to forgive those men, but she refused to let the past continue to poison her present or future. Interestingly, from that moment of forgiveness on, she was able to enjoy a healthy relationship with her husband. She got down to the root to deal with the fruit.

He himself bore our sins in his body on the tree, so that we might die to sins and live for righteousness; by his wounds you have been healed.

1 PETER 2:24

Don't Collect Debts

O LIVE IN THE PRESENT MOMENT, we must forgive those people who have hurt us in the past. Too often, we try to collect our debts from other people. When somebody hurts us, we feel like they owe us. Somebody should pay for that pain we have suffered! So we take it out on other people even though they weren't involved.

But here's the problem: only God can pay that debt; other people can't do it. Moreover, you should not drag something that happened in the past into your relationships today. Don't punish your spouse, your children, your friends, or your coworkers for something in your past. Instead, turn it over to God and keep your heart free from bitterness and resentment.

Start Each Day *Afresh*

"In your anger do not sin": Do not let the sun go down while you are still angry.

EPHESIANS 4:26

SCRIPTURE INSTRUCTS US to put on a fresh new attitude every morning, especially in our family relationships. Don't let little things build up. Don't harbor unforgiveness and resentment. Don't allow bad attitudes to develop, even those that may seem insignificant to you, because over time that bitter attitude will build and end up causing you major problems. You've got to do your best to keep your own heart free and clean, or eventually anger and bitterness will show up and affect your relationships.

Each morning, forgive the people who have hurt you. Every morning, let go of your disappointments and setbacks. Each new morning, receive God's mercy and forgiveness for the mistakes you've made, and forgive others for the hurts they have inflicted on you. Today focus on your possibilities; focus on what you can change rather than what you cannot change.

Oh, give thanks to the LORD, for He is good! For His mercy endures forever.

1 CHRONICLES 16:34 NKJV

Receive His Mercy

WHAT'S DONE IS DONE, and you need to live accordingly. If you lost your temper yesterday, quit dwelling on it. You cannot undo that, so ask for forgiveness and then do better today. Was your boss rude to you? Let it go. Don't go to work tomorrow with a chip on your shoulder. It's a new day. You didn't get your promotion? Okay, God must have something better in store for you.

Be responsible for your words or actions. If you have done wrong, offended someone, or hurt somebody, you should seek that person's forgiveness. But if you're trying to fix something that you know there's no way to fix, and you've done everything you can do, you must simply leave that up to God. Receive His mercy and go out to live your best life now.

Get *Rid* of the Poison

Search me, O God, and know my heart; try me and know my anxious thoughts; and see if there be any hurtful way in me, and lead me in the everlasting way.

PSALM 139:23–24 NASB

YEARS AGO IN A REMOTE VILLAGE OF Africa, people were dying because their water supply from a fresh mountain stream, which was fed from a spring, was contaminated. Divers were shocked to discover that pigs had drowned and gotten stuck in the spring's opening, contaminating the crystal clear mountain spring water. The divers removed the dead pigs, and the water began to flow clean and pure once again.

Something similar takes place in our lives when we don't forgive and a root of bitterness takes hold, contaminating our soul. You need to get rid of the poison that is polluting your life. Deal with it this morning by forgiving anyone who has hurt you, and then choose to live today in freedom and freshness.

Whoever believes in me, as the Scripture has said, streams of living water will flow from within him.

JOHN 7:38

Living Water

WHEN WE REFUSE TO FORGIVE, bitterness poisons our soul. Worse yet, after a while, we accept it as part of our personality. We say, "Well, I'm just an angry person. I'm always sarcastic and edgy. This is who I am." No, that's not who you are. You were made to be a crystal clear stream. God created you in His image to enjoy life to the full, not to live with bitterness and resentment, polluted and putrefied yourself and contaminating everyone else with whom you have influence.

It doesn't matter how polluted the stream in your life may be right now. If you'll begin to forgive the people who have offended you, and release all those hurts and pains, that bitterness will leave and you'll begin to experience the joy, peace, and freedom God intended you to have.

Quick to *Forgive*

Let us draw near to God with a sincere heart in full assurance of faith, having our hearts sprinkled to cleanse us from a guilty conscience and having our bodies washed with pure water.

HEBREWS 10:22

IT IS USUALLY THE LITTLE STUFF that gets us in trouble. Maybe your spouse is not spending as much time with you as you'd like, and you can feel yourself starting to get resentful with your mate, sarcastic, cryptic, or unfriendly. Instead of forgiving quickly, letting go of the hurts and pains, we quietly bury them deep down inside our hearts and minds. We don't want to talk about the issue. We don't want to think about it. We want to ignore it and hope that it will go away. But it won't.

Don't let your heart get polluted. Be quick to forgive, and the joy of the Lord will burst forth within you like a fresh mountain spring.

So teach us to number our days, that we may gain a heart of wisdom.

PSALM 90:12 NKJV

Number Your Days

OUR TIME HERE ON THIS EARTH is so short. What a shame it would be to allow something that happened in the past to ruin one more day. If you get stuck in a traffic jam, which you can't undo, know that God is still in control. If somebody offends you, your attitude should be, *I'm not going to let it sour the rest of my day. No, I'm traveling light; I'm not going to carry any extra burdens.*

I've made up my mind to do my best to enjoy every single day. I may make mistakes; things may not always go my way. I may be disappointed at times, but I've made a decision that I'm not going to allow what does or doesn't happen to me to steal my joy and keep me from God's abundant life.

Start *Clean* Each Day

And Jesus said to her, "Neither do I condemn you; go and sin no more."

JOHN 8:11 NKJV

*W*HEN YOU GET UP IN THE MORNING, you may recall all the mistakes you made yesterday—the times you blew it, when you had a bad attitude, or when you were undisciplined. No, don't start your day off like that. Get up in the morning and say, "Father, I thank You that this is going to be a great day. I thank You that I have discipline, self-control; that I make good decisions. I may not have done what I could have yesterday, but that day's gone. I'm going to get up and do better today."

Any day you get up feeling guilty about yesterday, if you fail to correct it right then and there, is going to be ruined as well. You'll drag around depressed and defeated. Don't fall into that trap.

As far as the east is from the west,
so far has he removed our
transgressions from us.

PSALM 103:12

Forget What *God* Forgets

WHEN YOU MAKE MISTAKES, ask God for forgiveness and then move on, confident that the moment you ask, God forgives you. Not only does God forgive you, but He chooses not to remember your mistakes. If somebody keeps bringing up negative incidents from your past, you know that's not God. Furthermore, He doesn't even keep a record of it. He's not going to flip back through His files and say, "Oh, wait a minute. I found something back there in 2005. I can't bless you."

No, as far as God is concerned, you don't even have a past. It's forgiven and gone. You are ready for a great present and a bright future. God let go of the past. The question is: will you let it go? Will you quit remembering what God has chosen to forget?

The God of *Another* Chance

If we confess our sins, He is faithful and righteous to forgive us our sins and to cleanse us from all unrighteousness.

1 JOHN 1:9 NASB

THE OLD TESTAMENT records how King David ordered a man murdered so he could marry his wife. But when David repented, God forgave him and still used him in a great way. A man named Saul hated and persecuted Christians and had them thrown in jail. Yet God forgave him, changed his name to Paul, and he ended up writing almost half the New Testament.

We all make mistakes, but God does not disqualify us simply because we have failed. He's the God of another chance. You may have missed plan A for your life, but God has a plan B, a plan C, a plan D, and a plan E. God will always find a way to get you to your final destination if you will trust Him.

*...to bestow on them a crown of
beauty instead of ashes, the oil
of gladness instead of mourning,
and a garment of praise instead
of a spirit of despair.*

ISAIAH 61:3

Beauty for Ashes

MY FATHER MARRIED YOUNG, and sadly, the marriage ended in a divorce. His dreams were shattered over his bad choices, and he didn't think he'd ever preach or marry again. He could have given up on fulfilling his God-given destiny. But Daddy made a decision to receive God's mercy, and little by little God restored his life and ministry, and eventually he fell in love and remarried. He pastored Lakewood Church in Houston for more than forty years, and today all five of my parents' children are working in the ministry. God took what the enemy meant for evil, and He turned it around and used it for good.

God gave Daddy beauty for his ashes, and He can do the same for you.

Shake Off the Doldrums

When we heard of it, our hearts melted and everyone's courage failed because of you, for the LORD your God is God in heaven above and on the earth below.

JOSHUA 2:11

RAHAB WAS A prostitute living in Jericho, yet she put her faith in God and confessed it to the Jewish spies, and God used her to help the children of Israel win a mighty victory (see Joshua 2). She could have easily felt too guilty and condemned to step forward. But while she couldn't do anything about her past, she could and did do something about her present moment to help the spies.

Nobody is too far gone, no matter what she or he has done. Maybe you've made some serious mistakes, and now you're living in guilt or with a sense of disqualification. God still loves you and has not run out of mercy. Ask for forgiveness and then move on. God can accomplish His great plan for you.

Arise, shine; for your light has come, and the glory of the LORD has risen upon you.

ISAIAH 60:1 NASB

Evict That Victim Mentality

OO MANY PEOPLE NOWADAYS are living with a victim mentality. They are so focused on what they've been through, complaining about how unfair it was, they don't realize they are dragging the pains of the past into the present. It's almost as though they get up each day and fill a big wheelbarrow with junk from the past and bring it into the new day.

Let go of that stuff! Your past does not have to poison your future. Just because you've been through some hurt and pain, or perhaps one or more of your dreams have been shattered, that doesn't mean God doesn't have another plan. God still has a bright future in store for you.

Live in the *Light*

For you were once darkness, but now you are light in the Lord. Live as children of light (for the fruit of the light consists in all goodness, righteousness and truth).

EPHESIANS 5:8–9

WE ALL WANT TO BE FREE from our past, and to do so you must understand this basic principle: the past is the past. You cannot undo anything that's happened to you. You can't relive one moment in the past. But you can do something about right now. Your attitude should be, *I refuse to dwell on the negative things that have happened to me. I'm not going to think about all that I've lost. I'm not going to focus on what could have been or should have been. This is a new day, and I'm going to start moving forward, knowing that God has a bright future in store for me.*

If you do that, God will give you a new beginning.

> *The Israelites grieved for Moses in the plains of Moab thirty days, until the time of weeping and mourning was over.*
>
> DEUTERONOMY 34:8

A *Victor's* Mentality

I N THE OLD TESTAMENT, when the people were going through mourning or some kind of loss, they marked their foreheads with ashes to signify their sorrow. This type of mourning was permissible and expected. Interestingly, God's people were allowed to grieve for a certain period of time, then God told them to move on with their lives.

It's the same way with us. When we go through some sort of loss or disappointment, God doesn't expect us to be emotionless. It's okay to go through a time of grieving. But don't allow yourself to live there. Don't let that season of mourning turn into a lifestyle of mourning, living a sour and negative life, going around with a chip on your shoulder. God wants to turn all that around. Start having a victor mentality this morning.

Get *Out* of the Ashes

Moses My servant is dead. Now therefore, arise, go over this Jordan, you and all this people, to the land which I am giving to them— the children of Israel.

JOSHUA 1:2 NKJV

*I*N THE BIBLE, a good man named Job suddenly lost his family, his health, and his business. Not surprisingly, in the midst of all that personal tragedy, Job didn't make good choices—at least, not at first. In fact, Job sat down among the ashes (see Job 2:8).

Are you sitting in some ashes of defeat today? Are you still sour because you didn't get that last promotion? Is your attitude negative because you weren't able to buy that house or car you really wanted? Are you bitter because a relationship didn't work out, or angry because you were treated abusively as you were growing up? Quit mourning over something that's already over and done. This is a new day. Your future can start right now.

Wake up, O sleeper, rise from the dead,
and Christ will shine on you.

EPHESIANS 5:14

Christ Is Shining

I TALKED TO A YOUNG WOMAN whose parents couldn't afford to send her to college, then her scholarship fell through, and she couldn't get the finances she needed. Now she was working at a job she didn't like, and the poison was coming out of her. She was so bitter and negative, it was destroying her future. I told her, "You've got to let all that go before anything's going to change. You've got to quit thinking about it, quit talking about it, quit rehearsing it all the time. The enemy would love to keep you negative and sour for the rest of your life."

If you've made that mistake, the good news is, God wants to take those negative experiences and use them to your advantage, if you'll dare to do your part and rise up.

Forward Not Backward

They followed the stubborn inclinations of their evil hearts. They went backward and not forward.

JEREMIAH 7:24

THE APOSTLE PAUL WAS full of fire and brought this attitude into his everyday life: *I'm forgetting what lies behind, and I'm pressing forward* (see Philippians 3:13). I recommend you adopt the same attitude this morning. Shake off the ashes of yesterday's discouragements and disappointments and say to yourself, "I'm throwing away my rearview mirror. I'm not looking back anymore at the mistreatment or the times when I got the short end of the stick. I'm not looking to the left or to the right. I'm looking straight ahead. I'm pressing forward, knowing God has good things in store for me."

Nobody can put God's fire in your soul. I can encourage you. Your friends can cheer you on. But it's not going to do any good until you put your foot down and make a decision to move forward with God.

He that covereth his sins shall not prosper: but whoso confesseth and forsaketh them shall have mercy.

PROVERBS 28:13 KJV

Forgive for Your Own Sake

A FEW DECADES AGO, several American companies authorized by the U.S. government attempted to bury toxic-waste products underground. They filled large metal drums, sealed them tightly, and buried them deep down below the topsoil. Within a short time, however, containers began to leak and the toxic waste seeped to the surface, causing terrible problems—killing vegetation, ruining water supplies, and forcing people to move. What went wrong? They tried to bury something that was so powerful that it was too toxic for the containers to hold. Had they disposed of them properly in the first place, they wouldn't have had this terrible problem.

It's the same with us when it comes to unforgiveness. We must forgive or else its toxic poison will continue to contaminate our life.

Guard Your *Heart*

Keep thy heart with all diligence; for out of it are the issues of life.

PROVERBS 4:23 KJV

RATHER THAN LETTING GO OF the hurt and pain we've experienced, too many of us attempt to bury it deep down inside our hearts. We attempt to cram unforgiveness, resentment, anger, and other destructive responses into our "leak-proof" containers, but one day the things you have tamped into your subconscious or buried deeply in the recesses of your heart will rise to the surface. We can't live with poison inside us and not expect it to eventually do us harm.

Forgiveness is the key to being free from toxic bitterness. Forgive the people who hurt you. Forgive the boss who did you wrong. Forgive the friend who betrayed you. Forgive the parent who mistreated you when you were younger. Don't let the root of bitterness grow deeper and continue to contaminate your life.

But the LORD replied, "Have you any right to be angry?"

JONAH 4:4

Deal with the Inside

W HAT DOES THE TOXIC WASTE of unforgiveness look like in our lives? For some people, it seeps out as anger. In other people, it smells like depression. For others, it reeks of low self-esteem. It can show up in many different ways, sometimes doing damage before we even realize it has reappeared. The simple truth is that if we have bitterness on the inside, it's going to end up contaminating everything that comes out of us. It will contaminate our personalities and our attitudes, as well as how we treat other people.

If you are harboring anger, ask yourself why. If you're always negative—about yourself, about others, about life in general—dare to ask yourself why this is. You must deal with the inside first, then you can really be happy. Then you can experience true, untainted, unalloyed victory in your life.

Forgive to Be Free

Be kind to one another, tender-hearted, forgiving each other, just as God in Christ also has forgiven you.

EPHESIANS 4:32 NASB

*I*F YOU WANT TO LIVE YOUR best life now, you must be quick to forgive. You need to forgive so you can be free, out of bondage, and happy. When we forgive, we're not doing it just for the other person; we're doing it for our own good. When we hold on to unforgiveness and live with grudges in our hearts, all we're doing is building walls of separation. We think we're protecting ourselves, but we're not. We are simply shutting other people out of our lives. We become isolated, alone, warped, and imprisoned by our own bitterness. Those walls don't merely keep people out; those walls keep us penned in.

You must forgive the people who hurt you so you can get out of prison. Forgiveness is a choice, but it is not an option.

It is for freedom that Christ has set us free. Stand firm, then, and do not let yourselves be burdened again by a yoke of slavery.

GALATIANS 5:1

Totally *Forgive*

IN 1973, RUDY TOMJANOVICH played NBA basketball for the Houston Rockets. In the middle of a close game, a fight broke out, and Rudy ran at full speed to try to break it up. Just as he got there, a player whipped around and swung as hard as he could—a punch that fractured Rudy's skull, broke his nose and cheekbones, and nearly killed him. It was months before he recovered.

When asked if he had forgiven the other player, Rudy said immediately, "Absolutely. I've totally forgiven him…. I knew if I wanted to move on with my life, I had to let it go. I didn't do it for him. I did it for me. I did it so I could be free."

True Freedom

For if you forgive men when they sin against you, your heavenly Father will also forgive you. But if you do not forgive men their sins, your Father will not forgive your sins.

MATTHEW 6:14–15

DO YOU REALIZE THAT WALLS of unforgiveness in your life prevent God's blessings from pouring into your life? Those walls can stop the flow of God's favor and keep your prayers from being answered. They'll keep your dreams from coming to pass. You must tear down the walls. You'll never be free until you do. Let go of those wrongs others have done to you. Get that bitterness out of your life. That's the only way you're going to truly be free.

You may experience genuine physical and emotional healing as you search your heart and are willing to forgive. You may see God's favor in a fresh, new way. You'll be amazed at what can happen when you release all that poison.

And the LORD restored Job's losses when he prayed for his friends. Indeed the LORD gave Job twice as much as he had before.

JOB 42:10 NKJV

Restoration Through Forgiveness

WHEN I WAS GROWING UP, a man attended our church whose hands were so crippled with arthritis, he could hardly use them. But one day he heard my father preaching about forgiveness, and how the lack of forgiveness keeps God's power from operating in our lives and prevents our prayers from being answered. He began asking God to help him get rid of anger and resentment in his heart toward those people who had hurt him over the years. As he forgave, the most amazing thing began to happen. One by one, his fingers straightened, and eventually, God restored his hands to normal.

You may see your prayers answered more quickly as you let go of the past and rid yourself of bitterness and resentment.

Check *Your* Heart

Make this your common practice: Confess your sins to each other and pray for each other so that you can live together whole and healed.

JAMES 5:16 THE MESSAGE

*W*HEN MY MOTHER discovered that she had cancer in 1981, she first made sure she didn't have any unforgiveness in her heart. She sat down and wrote letters to her friends and family, asking us to forgive her if she had ever done any wrong toward us. She wanted to make sure that nothing would interfere with God's healing power flowing into her.

This morning, you may have issues to deal with or people you need to forgive. You can ignore what you know to be true and keep allowing it to poison you and those around you. Or, you can make a much better choice by getting it out in the open and asking God to help you to totally forgive and let it all go.

Some trust in chariots and some in horses, but we trust in the name of the LORD our God.

PSALM 20:7

Trust God for Justice

BEING CHEATED IN A BUSINESS DEAL, betrayed by a friend, walked out on by a loved one—certainly, these kinds of losses leave indelible scars, causing you to want to hold on to your grief. It would be logical for you to seek revenge. Many people would even encourage you to do so. The slogan "Don't get mad, get even!" is a commonly accepted principle in America today.

But that is not God's plan for you. The Bible says, "God is a just God and He will settle and solve the cases of His people" (see Hebrews 10:30). If you want to live your best life now, you must learn to trust God to bring about the justice in your life. Turn matters over to Him and let Him handle them His way.

Doing *Right* when It Hurts

Beloved, never avenge yourselves, but leave the way open for [God's] wrath; for it is written, Vengeance is Mine, I will repay (requite), says the Lord.

ROMANS 12:19 AMP

GOD HAS PROMISED THAT if you will put your trust in Him to bring about the justice in your life, He will pay you back for all the unfair things that have happened to you (see Isaiah 61:7–9). That means you don't have to go around trying to pay everybody back for the wrong things they have done to you. God is your vindicator. Let Him fight your battles for you.

When you truly understand that you don't have to fix everything that happens to you, you don't have to try to manipulate the situation or control the circumstances or people involved. When you leave it up to God to pay you back, you take the high road, respond in love, and watch what God will do. Remember, God always pays back abundantly.

> *The LORD will vindicate His people, and will have compassion on His servants.*
>
> DEUTERONOMY 32:36 NASB

Let *God* Vindicate You

A FEW YEARS AGO, somebody dealt unethically with Victoria and me in a business deal, cheating us out of a lot of money. We resisted the temptation to pay him back and make him suffer. It was difficult to turn the matter over to God, and we had to keep reminding ourselves that God is a God of justice. This process continued for several years, and we didn't see any change.

One day, out of the clear blue, God supernaturally not only moved that man out of our lives, but He paid us back in abundance for everything he had taken. Sadly, the man who tried to cheat us eventually lost everything. And I certainly don't wish that on anybody, but that, too, is the justice of God. We eventually reap what we sow.

True Justice

In your patience possess ye your souls.
LUKE 21:19 KJV

*I*F YOU TRY TO BRING JUSTICE upon people who have done you wrong, you are closing the door for God to do it. Either you can do it God's way, or you can do it your way. If you tell yourself you're going to show them what you're made of, that attitude will prevent God from avenging you His way. God can bring true justice into your life, if you totally turn it over to Him.

Maybe you've been involved in a situation for months or even years, and now you're wondering, *Is God ever going to bring about justice? Does He even care?* Don't give up! Keep doing the right thing. God is building character in you, and you are passing that test. Remember, the greater the struggle, the greater the reward. Trust God to bring justice in His timing, not yours.

Blessed is the man who perseveres under trial, because when he has stood the test, he will receive the crown of life that God has promised to those who love him.

JAMES 1:12

Respect and Honor

WHEN DAVID WAS JUST A YOUNG MAN, he was anointed by the prophet Samuel to be the next king of Israel. Not long after that, he defeated the giant Goliath, and he became an instant hero throughout the land. People loved him, and his popularity ratings soared off the charts. But King Saul became extremely jealous of David and tried to kill him. David had to flee to the mountains, going from cave to cave, month after month.

Ironically, David hadn't done anything wrong. Rather than rebel and take matters into his own hands, David continued to treat Saul with respect and honor. Doing what's right doesn't mean it won't have a cost that goes with it.

Respect for Authority

May the LORD judge between you and me. And may the LORD avenge the wrongs you have done to me, but my hand will not touch you.

1 SAMUEL 24:12

WHEN DAVID SUFFERED unfairly at the hands of King Saul, he could easily have gotten bitter. He could have said, "God, I thought You chose me to be king. What's going on here?" But David didn't do that. He kept a good attitude, refusing to hurt Saul, even when he had the opportunity. Although Saul wasn't treating him right, David still respected Saul's position of authority.

It's easy to respect those in positions of authority as long as they are being kind to us or when we agree with them. But the true test comes when you get a "Saul" in your life, when somebody treats you unfairly for no apparent reason. If you will keep the right attitude, God will promote you at the proper time.

The Lord is good to those who depend on him, to those who search for him.

LAMENTATIONS 3:25 NLT

Overcoming Disappoint- ments

ONE OF THE MOST IMPORTANT KEYS TO moving forward into the great future God has for you is learning how to overcome the disappointments in your life. Because disappointments can pose such formidable obstacles to letting go of the past, you need to be sure you have dealt with this area before taking the next step to living at your full potential.

Often, defeating disappointments and letting go of the past are the flip side of the same coin, especially when you are disappointed in yourself. When you do something wrong, don't hold on to it and beat yourself up about it. Admit it, seek forgiveness, and move on. Be quick to let go of your mistakes and failures, hurts, pains, and sins. Don't let your setbacks become your identity.

Keep Trusting

The secret things belong to the LORD our God, but the things revealed belong to us and to our children forever, that we may follow all the words of this law.

DEUTERONOMY 29:29

ALL OF US FACE DISAPPOINTMENTS from time to time. No matter how much faith you have or how good a person you are, sooner or later, something (or somebody!) will shake your faith to its foundations. It may be something simple, such as not qualifying for a loan to buy that house you really wanted. Or it may be something more serious—a marriage relationship falling apart, the death of a loved one, or an incurable, debilitating illness. Whatever it is, that disappointment possesses the potential to derail you and wreck your faith.

Recognize in advance that disappointments will come. Be prepared to trust God when they do.

The LORD himself goes before you and will be with you; he will never leave you nor forsake you. Do not be afraid; do not be discouraged.

DEUTERONOMY 31:8

Hurts *Will* Hurt

DISAPPOINTMENTS almost always accompany setbacks. If you lose your job, most likely you are going to experience a strong sense of disappointment. If you go through a broken relationship, that's going to hurt. If you lose a loved one, there's a time of grieving, a time of sorrow. That is normal and to be expected.

When you suffer loss, nobody expects you to be an impenetrable rock or an inaccessible island in the sea. Not even God expects you to be so tough that you simply ignore the disappointments in life, shrugging them off as though you are impervious to pain. No, when we experience failure or loss, it's natural to feel remorse or sorrow. That's the way God made us. Just trust Him to be with you through it.

Faith Is *Present* Tense

They will come and shout for joy on the heights of Zion; they will rejoice in the bounty of the LORD—the grain, the new wine and the oil, the young of the flocks and herds. They will be like a well-watered garden, and they will sorrow no more.

JEREMIAH 31:12

WHEN YOU SUFFER LOSS and failure, it's natural to feel remorse or sorrow. That's the way God made us. But you must make a decision that you are going to move on. It won't happen automatically. You will have to rise up and say, "I don't care how hard this is, I am not going to let this get the best of me."

Don't live in regret or remorse or sorrow. They will only interfere with your faith. Faith must always be a present-tense reality, not a distant memory. God will turn those disappointments around. He will take your scars and turn them into stars for His glory.

O Lord, . . . Why then do you tolerate the treacherous? Why are you silent while the wicked swallow up those more righteous than themselves?

HABAKKUK 1:12–13

Grief for a *Season*

THE ENEMY LOVES TO DECEIVE US INTO wallowing in self-pity, fretting, feeling sorry for ourselves, or having a chip on our shoulders. "Why did this happen to me?" "God doesn't answer my prayers." "Why did my marriage end in divorce?" "Why did my business not succeed?" "Why did I lose my loved one?" "Why didn't things work out in my life?"

Such questions may be valid and may even be helpful to consider for a season, but if you are still grieving and feeling sorrow over a disappointment that took place a year or more ago, something is wrong! You are hindering your future. Quit wasting your time trying to figure out something you can't change. It's time to move on and start living your best life now.

God Has *Another* Plan

Thus says the LORD, "Restrain your voice from weeping and your eyes from tears; for your work will be rewarded," declares the LORD, "and they will return from the land of the enemy. There is hope for your future," declares the LORD.

JEREMIAH 31:16–17 NASB

SOMETIMES, NO MATTER how hard we pray, things don't turn out as we had hoped. Some are praying for their marriages to be restored; others are asking God to heal a rift between coworkers. I encourage people to persevere, to continue praying and believing for good things to happen. But we must also understand that God will not change another person's will. He has given every human being free will to choose whether to do right or wrong.

You may be heartbroken over a failed relationship or a bankrupt business, but don't carry around all that hurt and pain year after year. Don't let rejection fester inside you. God has something new in store for you.

See, I have placed before you an open door that no one can shut.

REVELATION 3:8

Disappointments into *Reappointments*

WHEN GOD ALLOWS ONE DOOR to close, He will open another door for you, revealing something bigger and better. The Bible says that God will take the evil the enemy brings into our lives, and He'll turn it around and use it for our good (see Genesis 50:20). He wants to take those disappointments and turn them into reappointments. But understand, whether you will experience all those good things depends to a large extent on your willingness to let go of the past.

Never put a question mark where God has put a period. Quit living in a negative frame of mind, stewing about something that is over and done. Focus on what you can change, rather than what you cannot. Shake yourself out of that "should have, could have, would have" mentality, and don't let the regrets of yesterday destroy the dreams of tomorrow.

God of Restoration

He makes me lie down in green pastures, he leads me beside quiet waters, he restores my soul.

PSALM 23:2–3

YOU CAN'T DO ANYTHING about what's gone, but you can do a great deal about what remains. You may have made some poor choices that have caused you awful heartache and pain. Perhaps you feel that your life is beyond repair. You may feel disqualified from God's best, convinced that you must settle for second best the rest of your life.

Worse yet, perhaps it was somebody else's foolish decisions that caused you to experience wrenching heartache and pain. Regardless, you must stop dwelling on it. Forgive the person who caused you the trouble and start clean right where you are this morning. If you continue to dwell on those past disappointments, you will block God's blessings in your life today. It's simply not worth it. Beyond that, God desires your restoration even more than you do!

The Lord said to Samuel, How long will you mourn for Saul, seeing I have rejected him from reigning over Israel?

1 SAMUEL 16:1 AMP

How Long?

A T GOD'S DIRECTION, Samuel had declared Saul to be the king of Israel. Then Samuel did his best to help Saul be a good king. Unfortunately, Saul disobeyed God, and God eventually rejected him as the king. Samuel was devastated and disappointed. But as Samuel was nursing his wounded heart, God asked him how long he was going to mourn over Saul.

Maybe you've invested a lot of time, effort, money, emotion, and energy in a relationship; you did your best to make it work out. But for some reason, it failed, and you feel robbed. Perhaps God is asking you a similar question today: "How long are you going to mourn over your broken dreams?" When we focus on our disappointments, we stop God from bringing fresh, new blessings into our lives.

A *Fresh* Attitude

The LORD said to Samuel, "...Fill your horn with oil and be on your way; I am sending you to Jesse of Bethlehem. I have chosen one of his sons to be king."

1 SAMUEL 16:1

GOD GAVE CLEAR INSTRUCTIONS to Samuel: "If you will quit mourning over Saul and get going, I'll show you a new, better beginning." Yes, Saul was God's first choice, but God always has another plan. Notice what God told Samuel to do: "Fill your horn with oil." Have a fresh new attitude. Put a smile on your face. Get the spring back in your step and be on your way.

If Samuel had wallowed in his disappointment, he might have missed King David, one of the greatest kings in the Bible. Similarly, we risk missing out on the new things God wants to do in our lives. It's time to get going!

He who was seated on the throne said,
"I am making everything new!"

REVELATION 21:5

Everything *New*

I KNOW A MAN WHO lost his beautiful wife in a tragic auto accident more than ten years ago, and he's still grieving today! I tried to encourage him, but he constantly made excuses, blaming God, blaming other people. I realized that he didn't really want to get well. He liked the attention that it got him. He became known as "the man who lost his wife." He even had several newspaper articles about that accident lying on his coffee table to remind him of the pains of the past. Sadly, he let his tragedy become his identity. To this day he is living a depressed and defeated life. He allowed a season of mourning to turn into a lifetime of mourning.

God wants to give us new beginnings, but He can't until we let go of the old.

Clothed with *Joy*

You have turned my mourning into dancing for me; You have put off my sackcloth and girded me with gladness.

PSALM 30:11 AMP

MANY INDIVIDUALS SPEND THEIR LIVES looking in their rearview mirrors thinking about what could have been, what should have been, always dwelling on the pains of yesterday. If you've had unfair things happen to you, you must make a decision today that you're going to let all that go or it will interfere with God's doing good things in your life.

The Scripture says that God wants to give us beauty for our ashes, joy for our mourning (see Isaiah 61:1–3). But here's the key: you have to let go of the ashes before God can give you the beauty. Ashes represent what's left over after something's been burned up—our broken dreams, our disappointments, our hurts, our failures. We all have our share of ashes, and God wants to give us beauty in exchange for them.

*I pour out my complaint before him;
before him I tell my trouble.*

PSALM 142:2

Fresh, *New* Dreams

WHEN YOU ARE TEMPTED TO sit around feeling sorry for yourself, complaining about how unfair life is, ask yourself a tough question: "Do I really want to get well, or have I gotten comfortable with where I am in life?" Don't ever let your setback become your identity. To put it bluntly, you've got to get over that. Quit talking about it. Quit opening up that old wound time and time again. You may have been severely wounded by a divorce; it's time to let it go. Move on. Quit mourning about something you can't change.

You must let go of your shattered dreams if you want God to give you fresh, new dreams. Quit dwelling on your disappointments. Forgive the people who have hurt you. Release any remaining bitterness, and then God will give you a new beginning.

Dwell on the *Positive*

Your beginnings will seem humble, so prosperous will your future be.

JOB 8:7

*G*OD IS ALWAYS WANTING to do something new in your life as well as to rid you of the old. We need to avoid dwelling on things that remind us of the pains of the past, that evoke a negative, hurtful memory. In my case, for instance, I don't go to my father's gravesite, because I don't want to bring up those memories of my dad. Rather, we have pictures in our house of Daddy with my children, things that bring back happy memories. Certainly, if going to a loved one's gravesite brings you peace, fine. But if it's opening up all those old wounds, don't do it. That's not healthy.

Friend, God always has a new beginning. The real question is: are you willing to move on with your life with a good attitude, knowing that God has a bright future in store?

The LORD is my shepherd, I shall not be in want.

PSALM 23:1

Find *Strength* Through Adversity

YOU MAY BE EXPERIENCING some sort of adversity in your life today. Someone close to you may be hard to get along with. You don't like your job, or maybe you have other obstacles in your path. Regardless of what's going on in your life, understand this: the tough times of life cause us to grow; that's when our faith is stretched. That's when God is doing a work in us. It may be uncomfortable. We may not like it, but if we can keep the right attitude, God has promised to use that difficulty for our good. He'll use it for our advantage.

Our attitude in adversity should be, *God, I know You're in complete control of my life, and You've got me exactly where You want me to be, so I'm going to stay filled with faith.*

Stand Firm

Be on your guard; stand firm in the faith; be men of courage; be strong.

1 CORINTHIANS 16:13

YOUR FAITH IS SIMILAR TO a muscle. It grows stronger through resistance. It is exercised when it's being stretched, when it's being pushed. That's why God does not usually deliver us from adversity or uncomfortable situations overnight. He uses those times to build our "spiritual muscles."

Some people live in despair and disappointment, all because their circumstances are not exactly what they desire them to be. They are never happy unless everything is going their way, everybody is treating them right, and they are immune from experiencing discomfort. In other words, they never are happy! Besides, that's a very shallow way to live. And, if you lose your joy every time something negative happens to you, the enemy will make sure you always have somebody or something in your life that's going to keep you sour. But don't make that mistake.

Consider it pure joy, my brothers, whenever you face trials of many kinds, because you know that the testing of your faith develops perseverance.

JAMES 1:2–3

Tests of Your Faith

YOU MAY HAVE A thousand difficult reasons why you could be unhappy, but don't slip into that trap. Choose to enjoy each day in spite of your circumstances. Every day you live with a negative attitude, dominated by your discouragements, is a day you've wasted. And what a shame to waste what God has given us!

Understand, adversities are simply a test of your faith. Perhaps God wants to see how you will treat other people when you are mistreated. What kind of attitude are you going to have if your prayers aren't answered quickly? Our characters develop in the tough times. Something happens on the inside; God is causing us to grow up. If He delivered us instantaneously from every problem, we'd never develop into the persons He really wants us to be.

God's *Refining* Fire

Beloved, do not be surprised at the fiery ordeal among you, which comes upon you for your testing, as though some strange thing were happening to you.

1 PETER 4:12 NASB

WHEN ADVERSITY COMES KNOCKING on the door, some people immediately think they have done something wrong, that God surely must be punishing them. Friend, God will not allow a difficulty to come into your life unless He has a purpose for it. Granted, there are times when we can't understand what we're going through or why, but we must learn to believe that God is going to bring good out of it.

God says, "Don't think it's a big deal when you go through these tough times." Learn to cooperate with God and be quick to change and correct the areas He brings to light. Then you'll pass that test and you will be promoted to a new level.

He cuts off every branch in me that bears no fruit, while every branch that does bear fruit he prunes so that it will be even more fruitful.

JOHN 15:2

Keep *Changing*

I'VE DISCOVERED THAT GOD IS more interested in changing me than He is in changing my circumstances. I'm not saying that God won't deliver us from our struggles by changing the circumstances. But most of the time, God uses adversities to bring to light impurities in our characters or areas in which we need to improve. God deliberately uses some situations as a mirror, so we can recognize the problem in ourselves and learn to deal with it. He's working something out of us so we can be the people He really wants us to be.

God may use people, such as your spouse or children, and situations in your life to be the unwitting mirrors that reveal areas where you need to change. Take a good look, and make the necessary changes.

Iron *Sharpens* Iron

As iron sharpens iron, so one man sharpens another.

PROVERBS 27:17

ERHAPS YOU CAN'T STAND someone in your life, and you wonder when God is going to change them. Have you considered that to change you God may have purposely arranged for you to be in close proximity to that person? He may be trying to toughen you up a little and teach you to have some endurance, to not run from everything that is hard, uncomfortable, or inconvenient.

God is not going to change anyone you are dealing with until He first changes you. But if you'll quit complaining about everybody around you and, instead, start taking a good look inside and working with God to change you, God will change those other people. Begin today to examine your own heart and see if there are attitudes and motives that you need to change.

So be truly glad. There is wonderful joy ahead, even though you have to endure many trials for a little while.

1 PETER 1:6 NLT

Let God *Change* You

PERHAPS YOU ARE IN A TRIAL TODAY, and you are praying for God to deliver you out of that adverse situation. That is a legitimate prayer, but maybe you're missing the point of why you are being allowed to go through that trying time in the first place.

Recognize that God is molding you and refining you. You can pray, you can resist, you can bind, you can sing and shout, but it's not going to do any good if God's purpose is to change you. And the sooner you learn your lesson and start dealing with those bad attitudes and start ruling over your emotions, the quicker you'll go to the next level in your spiritual journey. We can't run from everything that's hard in our lives.

In the *Potter's* Hands

Yet, O LORD, you are our Father.
We are the clay, you are the potter;
we are all the work of your hand.

ISAIAH 64:8

PERHAPS YOU GET WORRIED and fearful when important things don't go your way. Have you ever thought that God may be allowing those events to teach you to trust Him and to see if you will stay peaceful and calm in the midst of the storm? He may be trying to toughen you up, to help you develop some backbone and stability in your life.

Clay works best when it is pliable, malleable, and moldable. But if you are hard, crusty, and set in your ways, God will have to pound away on that old hard clay to get out the lumps. Be willing to deal with any issues that God brings up. Work with Him in the refining process rather than fighting against Him.

Work out your own salvation.

PHILIPPIANS 2:12 NKJV

Work *It* Out

CERTAINLY, none of us enjoy going through struggles, but you have to understand that your struggle may be an opportunity for advancement and promotion. The very thing you are fighting against so tenaciously may be the springboard that catapults you to a new level of excellence. Your challenges may become your greatest assets.

Without the resistance of air, an eagle can't soar. Without the resistance of water, a ship can't float. Without the resistance of gravity, you and I can't even walk. Without opposition or resistance, there is no potential for progress. There are no shortcuts; there's no easy way to mature physically, emotionally, or spiritually. You must remain determined and work with God. Salvation is more than a onetime prayer. It is constantly cooperating with God, dealing with the issues He brings up, keeping a good attitude, and allowing Him to change you as He sees fit.

An *Attitude* of Gratitude

It is good to give thanks to the LORD and to sing praises to Your name, O Most High; to declare Your lovingkindness in the morning, and Your faithfulness by night.

PSALM 92:1–2 NASB

HAVE YOU EVER CONSIDERED that perhaps you are not getting your prayers answered because you are not grateful for what God has already done for you? The Scriptures teach us that we should continually give God thanks; we should live with an attitude of gratitude.

You may say, "I've been through so many disappointments. I lost my business last year. My marriage didn't work out. I've lost so much. How do you expect me to be grateful?" But if it had not been for the goodness of God, you could have lost it all. If not for God's mercy, you might not even be here today. Quit looking at what you have lost and start thanking God for what you have left.

But thanks be to God! He gives us the victory through our Lord Jesus Christ.

1 CORINTHIANS 15:57

Thanks Be to God

*M*Y FRIEND FREDDIE LAMB was on the side of the freeway changing a flat tire when a drunk driver smashed his car into him. As a result of the incident, Freddie lost both of his legs beneath the knees. Several days after the accident, my parents went to the hospital to visit Freddie, thinking that he would be distraught and upset over his loss. But all Freddie could talk about was how God had spared his life. Freddie wasn't focused on what he didn't have. He was thanking God for what he did have. Today, Freddie Lamb has new artificial limbs, and everywhere he goes, he tells people what God has done for him.

Make a decision today that no matter what comes against you, you're going to have a grateful attitude. You're going to find some reason to give God thanks.

Look for What's *Right*

Do everything without complaining or arguing, so that you may become blameless and pure, children of God…

PHILIPPIANS 2:14–15

MANY PEOPLE GO AROUND complaining, always looking at what's wrong. They see the negative in every situation, and then they wonder why they're not enjoying their lives. Really, it's because they have an ungrateful, unthankful attitude. It's a heart issue, and if they don't get to the root cause and start being more grateful, it's never going to change.

God didn't give us our mouths to complain. You may not have everything you would like today. In fact, you may be dealing with a lot of problems, but complaining is only going to make matters worse. Quit taking inventory of everything that's wrong, and start thanking God for what's right, for what God has already done or what He's already given. Until you have a grateful attitude, you're going to stay right where you are.

Let them sacrifice the sacrifices of thanksgiving, and declare His works with rejoicing.

PSALM 107:22 NKJV

Change Your Perspective

*Y*OUR LIFE MIGHT TAKE a radical turn for the better if you'd just change your perspective and start being more grateful. Remember this: no matter how many negative things you have in your life, somebody would love to trade places with you. You may not have the perfect job, but if you got laid off and couldn't pay your bills for six months, you'd be thrilled to have your old job.

We need to remind ourselves, "I may not like this job, but I am blessed to have it. I may not like this house I'm living in, but what would I do if I didn't have my home? I may not particularly enjoy the person to whom I'm married, but what would happen if one day that person was gone?" We need to see our circumstances in a different light.

A *Habit* of Giving Thanks

Now, our God, we give you thanks, and praise your glorious name.

1 CHRONICLES 29:13

SOME PARENTS PERPETUALLY complain about their children. "These children drive me nuts. They make such a mess." Do you realize that some husbands and wives have spent thousands of dollars and have gone through all kinds of medical procedures, trying to become pregnant and have children? They would give anything to be able to clean up that mess.

When you drive to work, when it's time to go to church, when you get out of bed in the morning, be thankful to God, no matter what you face. If you have fifteen dollars to your name, you are in the top 8 percent of the world's wealthiest people! We have so much to be grateful for. We should get in the habit of giving God thanks all day long. Start by giving Him thanks for this new morning.

...being continually built up in Him, becoming increasingly more confirmed and established in the faith, just as you were taught, and abounding and overflowing in it with thanksgiving.

COLOSSIANS 2:7 AMP

Enjoy "Normal" Life

IT'S EASY TO THINK, *I can't be happy. I don't have anything exciting going on.* But if your loved one got sick, or you lost your job, you would long for the mundane. You would long to get back to where you are right now. Why not make a decision to be grateful for what God has done in your life? Don't take "normal" life for granted. Don't wait until something is taken away before you really appreciate what you have.

Learn to enjoy what God has given you. Take time for the people you love. Quit working all the time. When you come to the end of your life, you will never regret having spent time with your family. Nobody ever says on their deathbed, "If I had to do it again, I'd spend more time at the office."

What *Matters* Most

Each man's life is but a breath.

PSALM 39:5

PEOPLE SAY TO ME, "Joel, I don't have enough time to get everything done as it is, let alone spend time with my family." That's true, but when you come to the end of your life, you're still going to have things to do. Your schedule will never slow down on its own. You must make time for what matters most. If you don't schedule time for the people you love, nobody will do it for you.

Without fail, people who have gone through life-threatening diseases all talk about the same thing—how much more they appreciate each day. They realize that every new sunrise is a gift from God. We need to realize that in a moment, we could be gone. We need to learn to live each day to the fullest, as though it could be our last.

Therefore do not worry about tomorrow, for tomorrow will worry about itself.

MATTHEW 6:34

Great Days

A YOUNG MAN WITH WHOM I used to play basketball started having a problem with his eye. He went to the doctor and was diagnosed as having cancer in the eye. Since it seemed a high probability that he was going to lose his vision, he was devastated. In surgery, the doctors discovered that rather than cancer, the problem was an extremely unusual fungus that they were able to remove and saved his vision. When the young man heard the good news, he said, "This is the greatest day of my life."

Think about it. He had simply received the news that he could continue to see. If you can see and hear, if you are healthy, if you have family and friends, if you've got a job, food, and a place to live, learn to appreciate those things. Thank God for all you have.

Praise Him

Enter his gates with thanksgiving and his courts with praise; give thanks to him and praise his name.

PSALM 100:4

I LIKE TO START OFF MY DAY by thanking God for the basics: "Father, thank You for my health. Thank You for my children. Thank You for my family. Thank You for my home. Father, thank You for all You've done for me." Even when I pray, most of my praying these days is simply giving God thanks.

Friend, God already knows your needs. He already knows what you're going to say before you say it. There's nothing wrong with asking God for things—the Scripture clearly instructs us to look to Him to meet our needs—but we should spend more time praising Him for His goodness than requesting His goodies. We should spend more time giving God thanks for what He's already done than we do asking Him to do new things.

I will extol the LORD at all times; his praise will always be on my lips.

PSALM 34:1

Extol the Lord

LIFE IS ALL ABOUT HOW YOU choose to see things. You can complain about your boss, or you can thank God for your job. You can complain about mowing the lawn, or you can thank God that you have a yard. You can complain about the price of gas, or you can thank God that you have an automobile.

Years ago, I was driving in a pouring rainstorm. I lost control of my car and spun out on the freeway, crashing into the guardrail and almost getting run over by a huge eighteen-wheeler. Amazingly, I came out of that crash without a scratch, but my car was wrecked. A friend thought I'd be upset about my car, but I was just grateful to be alive. I made up my mind to let His praise continually be in my mouth.

Keep Getting Up

Therefore, put on every piece of God's armor so you will be able to resist the enemy in the time of evil. Then after the battle you will still be standing firm.

EPHESIANS 6:13 NLT

LIVING YOUR BEST LIFE NOW is downright difficult sometimes. Many people give up far too easily when things don't go their way or they face some kind of adversity. Instead of persevering, they get all bent out of shape. Before long they're down and discouraged, which is understandable, especially when we've struggled with a problem or a weakness for a long time. It's not unusual to come to a place where we acquiesce.

But you have to be more determined than that. The good news is, you don't have to stay down. Even if you can't see up on the outside, get up on the inside. Have that victor's attitude and mentality. Stay with an attitude of faith. Keep on getting up in your heart, mind, and will.

The steps of a good man are ordered by the LORD: and he delighteth in his way. Though he fall, he shall not be utterly cast down: for the LORD upholdeth him with his hand.

PSALM 37:23–24 KJV

Set *Your* Face

*L*IVING AT OUR FULL POTENTIAL involves finding strength through adversity. Our circumstances in life may occasionally knock us down or force us to sit down for a while, but we must not stay down.

Set your face like a flint and say, "God, I may not understand this, but I know You are still in control. And You said all things would work together for my good. You said You would take this evil and turn it around and use it to my advantage. So Father, I thank You that You are going to bring me through this!" No matter what you may face in life, if you know how to get up on the inside, adversities cannot keep you down.

Don't Give Up

Look to the LORD and his strength; seek his face always.

PSALM 105:4

*Y*OU MAY HAVE RECEIVED a bad report from the doctor. Maybe you lost your largest client at work. Perhaps you just found out that your child is in trouble. You may be facing some other serious setback, and you feel as though life has caved in on top of you, knocking you off your feet and pushing you into the pits. You may be in a situation today where you have done your best. You've prayed and believed. You've placed your faith firmly on the truth of God's Word. But it just doesn't look like anything good is happening. Now you're tempted to say, "What's the use? It's never going to change."

Don't give up! Keep standing. Keep praying; keep believing; keep hoping in faith. "Don't cast away your confidence," the Bible teaches, "for payday is coming" (see Hebrews 10:35).

Be strong and let us fight bravely for our people and the cities of our God.

2 SAMUEL 10:12

Standing *Strong*

TALKED TO A MAN WHO had been making a good salary working in a prestigious position, but then suddenly he was let go. I was certain he was going to be distraught. But when he came to see me, he said, "Joel, I can't wait to see what God has in store for me next!" He had been knocked down, but he had a victor's mentality. His attitude was: *This thing is not going to defeat me or steal my joy. I know when one door closes, God will open up a bigger and better door.*

Today, you can say, "Even if the enemy hits me with his best shot, his best will never be good enough. When it's all said and done, when the smoke clears and the dust settles, I'm still going to be standing strong."

Encourage Yourself in the Lord

David was greatly distressed because the people spoke of stoning him, for all the people were embittered, each one because of his sons and his daughters, but David strengthened himself in the LORD his God.

1 SAMUEL 30:6 NASB

BEFORE DAVID BECAME KING of Israel, he and his men returned home to find their city had been attacked, their homes burned, their possessions stolen, and their women and children kidnapped. Instead of sitting around devastated and mourning over what had been lost, David encouraged himself in the Lord and convinced his men to attack the enemy. As they persevered, God supernaturally helped them to recover everything that had been stolen.

To live your best life now, you must act on your will, not simply your emotions. Sometimes that means you have to take steps of faith even when you are hurting, grieving, or still reeling from an attack of the enemy. Develop a victor's mentality and watch what God begins to do.

*Do not throw away your confidence;
it will be richly rewarded. You need
to persevere so that when you have
done the will of God, you will receive
what he has promised.*

HEBREWS 10:35–36

Persevere

THIS MORNING, you may be waiting for God to change your circumstances. *Then* you're going to be happy; *then* you're going to have a good attitude; *then* you're going to give God praise. But God is waiting for you to get up on the inside and take courage. It will definitely take determination, but you can do it.

God wants you to be a winner, not a whiner. Don't allow yourself to wave the white flag of surrender. Show the enemy that you're more determined than he is. Shout aloud if you must, "I'm going to stand in faith even if I have to stand my whole lifetime!" When you do your part, God will work supernaturally to change things in your life.

When the *Bottom* Drops Out

Your kingdom is an everlasting kingdom, and Your dominion endures throughout all generations. The LORD sustains all who fall and raises up all who are bowed down.

PSALM 145:13–14 NASB

RIEND, LIFE IS TOO SHORT TO TRUDGE through it depressed and defeated. No matter what has come against you or what is causing you to slip and fall, no matter who or what is trying to push you down, you need to keep getting up on the inside. We were not created to live in depression and defeat. A negative spirit dries up your energy; it weakens your immune system. Many people are living with physical ailments and emotional bondages because they are not standing up on the inside.

If you want to give your enemy a nervous breakdown, learn to keep a good attitude even when the bottom drops out! Learn to be happy even when things don't go your way. Stand strong and fight the good fight of faith.

Rejoice always; pray without ceasing;
in everything give thanks; for this is
God's will for you in Christ Jesus.

1 THESSALONIANS 5:16–18 NASB

A *Determined* Spirit

WHEN MANY PEOPLE FACE ADVERSITY, they allow their doubt to cloud their determination, thus weakening their faith. They don't persevere; they don't keep a good attitude. Ironically, because their spirits are not right, they remain in bad situations longer than necessary. Medical science tells us that people with a determined, feisty spirit get well quicker than people who are prone to be negative and discouraged. That's because God made us to be determined.

Get rid of the mind-set that's saying you can't do it; you can't be happy; you have too much to overcome. Those are all lies from the enemy. Learn to tap into the can-do power that God has placed inside you. Everyone has a reason to give God thanks, so rejoice and be glad.

Don't Back Down

Fight the good fight of the faith.
Take hold of the eternal life to which
you were called.

1 TIMOTHY 6:12

GROWING UP, my family had a big German shepherd named Scooter, and he was king of the neighborhood. Scooter was strong and fast and looked like he could fight a tiger. But one day a spunky Chihuahua raced out of a house toward Scooter, barking up a storm. The closer that little dog got, the more Scooter hung his head like a coward. When the Chihuahua finally got face-to-face with Scooter, Scooter just lay down, rolled over, and put all four legs up in the air.

We do something similar when we know that we have all God's resources at our disposal, but adversity barks and we roll over and say, "I quit. This is too tough." It's time to tap into God's power, stand up, and fight.

Because the Sovereign LORD helps me,
I will not be disgraced. Therefore have
I set my face like flint, and I know
I will not be put to shame.

ISAIAH 50:7

Through the Darkness

ARE YOU GOING THROUGH a dark time in your life? Perhaps somebody deceived you, took advantage of you, or mistreated you, and now you are tempted to sit around mourning over what you have lost, thinking about how unfair it was, and how your life will never be the same. You may be weary and tired, worn down, and ready to give up.

You must get out of that defeated mentality and start thinking and believing positively. There is no reason for you to be perpetually living "under the circumstances," always down, always discouraged. Your attitude should be: *I'm coming out of this thing!* No matter how many times you get knocked down, keep getting back up. God sees your resolve. He sees your determination. And when you do everything you can do, that's when God will step in and do what you can't do.

Trust *God's* Timing

For the vision is yet for an appointed time; but at the end it will speak, and it will not lie. Though it tarries, wait for it; because it will surely come, it will not tarry.

HABAKKUK 2:3 NKJV

*H*UMAN NATURE tends to want everything right now. When we pray for our dreams to come to pass, we want them to be fulfilled immediately. But we have to understand, God has an appointed time to answer our prayers and to bring our dreams to pass. And the truth is, no matter how badly we want it sooner, it's not going to change His appointed time.

We all have to wait and learn to trust God. The key is, are we going to wait with a good attitude and expectancy, knowing God is at work whether we can see anything happening or not? We need to rest assured that, behind the scenes, God is putting all the pieces together.

Let us then approach the throne of grace with confidence, so that we may receive mercy and find grace to help us in our time of need.

HEBREWS 4:16

God Is in Control

GOD IS NOT LIKE AN ATM MACHINE, where you punch in the right codes and receive what you requested. Prayers are not always answered within twenty-four hours. God often works the most when we see it and feel it the least.

When you misunderstand God's timing, you live upset and frustrated, wondering when God is going to do something. But when you understand God's timing, you won't live all stressed out. You can relax, knowing that God is in control, and at the "appointed time" He is going to make it happen. It may be next week, next year, or ten years from now. When it happens, you will see the culmination of everything that God has been doing.

No Need to Struggle

...for anyone who enters God's rest also rests from his own work, just as God did from his.

HEBREWS 4:10

WHEN YOU LIVE TRUSTING GOD, you really don't have to struggle. You can be at peace, knowing that at the right time, God will keep His promise—and it's not going to be one second late. If you're unmarried and are believing for a spouse, you don't have to beg God incessantly to send you a mate. If you are believing for your family members to develop a relationship with God, you don't have to shove the Bible down their throats. If you have some areas in your life in which you need to improve, you don't need to beat yourself up because you're not changing fast enough.

When you are truly living by faith, you can relax in the "rest" of God. In total trust, you know He will bring it into being.

But I trust in you, O Lord; I say,
"You are my God." My times are
in your hands.

PSALM 31:14–15

In *God's* Hands

*D*AVID HAD A BIG DREAM FOR HIS LIFE. He had a desire to make a difference, but as a young man he spent many years as a shepherd, caring for his father's sheep. I'm sure there were plenty of times when he was tempted to think that God had forgotten him. He must have thought, *God, what am I doing here? There's no future in this place. When are You going to change this situation?* But David understood God's timing. He knew that if he would be faithful in obscurity, God would bring his dreams to pass in due season.

You know the story. God promoted David out of those fields, he defeated Goliath, and eventually he was made king of Israel. Contentment starts in our attitude and is rewarded with patience.

Be Content

I have learned to be content whatever the circumstances.

PHILIPPIANS 4:11

PERHAPS YOU HAVE A BIG DREAM in your heart—a dream to have a better marriage, to own your own business, to help hurting people—but you don't really see any human way your dream could happen.

I have good news for you! God isn't limited to natural, human ways of doing things. If you're not seeing God move in your life right now, either your requests are not God's best and will probably not be answered the way you'd like, or it must not be the right time. If you will trust God and keep a good attitude, staying faithful right where you are and not getting in a hurry and trying to force things to happen, God will promote you at the right time, in your due season. He will bring your dreams to pass. Rest in Him!

"For my thoughts are not your thoughts, neither are your ways my ways," declares the LORD. "As the heavens are higher than the earth, so are my ways higher than your ways and my thoughts than your thoughts."

ISAIAH 55:8–9

God *Sees* the Big Picture

WE DON'T ALWAYS understand God's methods. His ways don't always make sense to us, but we have to realize that God sees the big picture. Consider this possibility: you may be ready for what God has for you, but somebody else who is going to be involved is not ready yet. God has to do a work in another person or another situation before your prayer can be answered according to God's will for your life. All the pieces have to come together for it to be God's perfect time.

To live your best life now, you must learn to trust God's timing. Let God do it His way. The answer will come, and it will be right on time.

At the *Proper* Time

Let us not become weary in doing good, for at the proper time we will reap a harvest if we do not give up.

GALATIANS 6:9

THIS MORNING, you may be frustrated because you feel God's plan isn't working in your life. But never fear; God is arranging all the pieces to come together to work out His plan for your life. Though you may not feel it or see it, He has been working in your favor long before you encountered the problem.

Don't grow impatient and try to force doors to open. Don't try to make things happen in your own strength. Your situation may look just as it did for the past ten years, but then one day, in a split second of time, God will bring it all together. When it is God's timing, all the forces of darkness can't stop Him. When it's your due season, God will bring it to pass.

In the world you have tribulation, but take courage; I have overcome the world.

JOHN 16:33 NASB

More *Blessed*

DVERSITIES AND HARDSHIPS are opportunities for us to go higher. Consequently, God does not prevent every negative thing from coming into our lives. "Unfair things will happen to you," Jesus said, "but here's the key: be of good cheer, for I have overcome the world."

Throughout the Scripture, God says if we'll keep the right attitude, if we'll stay full of joy and full of hope, even though He may not stop all the trouble, when we come out, we won't be the same as we were before. We'll be more blessed, healthy, and prosperous, better off than we were previously. None of us enjoys the pain. But we can stay filled with hope, knowing that God will never waste the pain. He will always use it to our advantage.

God *Can* Turn It Around

I will repay you for the years the locusts have eaten.

JOEL 2:25

THINK ABOUT JOSEPH. His brothers were so jealous of him, they sold him into slavery. Other young men his age, no doubt, were out having a good time, enjoying their lives. But Joseph was confined, living in a foreign land, having to work all the time. It was unfair; worse yet, Joseph's heartache and pain were caused by somebody else's poor choices and bad attitude.

But God saw that injustice. Somehow, some way, God can make up all those years. That's what He did for Joseph (see Genesis 41). Even though Joseph spent thirteen years in slavery and in prison, God made it all up to him, and he came out promoted and increased. He now had a position of honor as the prime minister of all Egypt, second in command only to Pharaoh. Because Joseph kept the right attitude, God brought him out much better than he was before.

Return to your fortress, O prisoners of hope; even now I announce that I will restore twice as much to you.

ZECHARIAH 9:12

Prisoners of *Hope*

SO MANY PEOPLE go around discouraged and defeated. They live with anger, resentment, and bitterness, rather than hope. "But Joel, you don't know what I've been through. You don't know how bad my marriage has been, or how deep I'm in debt."

Friend, quit dwelling on all of that. Don't magnify your problems. Magnify your God. The bigger you make God, the smaller your problems become, and the more faith will rise in your heart. God is keeping the records in your life as well. If somebody has mistreated you and done you wrong, don't sit around feeling sorry for yourself. Let hope fill your heart. Know that God will bring you out with twice what you had before. God will never waste anything that you go through.

Subject to Change

So we fix our eyes not on what is seen, but on what is unseen. For what is seen is temporary, but what is unseen is eternal.

2 CORINTHIANS 4:18

THE SCRIPTURE TEACHES that we shouldn't look at the things that are seen but at the things that are not seen; for the things that are seen are only temporary, but the things that are seen through our eyes of faith are eternal. One translation says, "The things that are seen are subject to change." That means your health or finances may not look too good today, but that's subject to change. Nothing may be going right in your life, but it's all subject to change.

When you look at your child who's not living right, instead of getting discouraged and losing your hope, look at him or her and say, "You are subject to change." Stay filled with hope, and start expecting things to change.

And, behold, the angel of the Lord came upon him, and a light shined in the prison.

ACTS 12:7 KJV

Suddenly

IF YOU WANT TO SEE GOD restore what's been stolen from you, get up each morning expecting good things to happen. You need to know that in a moment of time, God could turn it all around. Suddenly you could get your miracle. Suddenly God could bring someone new into your life. Suddenly you could get that promotion. All it takes is one "suddenly." In a split second, with one touch of God's favor, everything can change.

Put your faith out there and remind yourself that God wants to restore good things back to you. Our attitude should be, *I'm not going to sit around mourning over what I've lost. I may have been knocked down, but I'm going to get back up again, knowing that Almighty God is on my side, and if God be for me, who dares be against me?*

When *Life* Doesn't Make Sense

After Job had prayed for his friends, the LORD made him prosperous again and gave him twice as much as he had before.... The LORD blessed the latter part of Job's life more than the first.

JOB 42:10, 12

JOB WAS A GOOD MAN who loved God. Yet he lost his business, his flocks and herds, his family, and his health. Things could not get any worse for Job, and I'm sure he was tempted to be bitter. He could have said, "God, it's not fair. I don't understand why this is happening to me."

But no, Job knew God could turn any situation around. And his attitude was, *Even if I die, I'm going to die trusting God. I'm going to die believing for the best.* And, when it was all said and done, God not only turned Job's calamity around, He brought Job out with twice that he had before.

But he knows the way that I take;
when he has tested me, I will come
forth as gold.

JOB 23:10

Sustaining Faith

ESTERDAY MORNING, you read about Job. Not only did he lose his children, his wealth, and his health, but his own wife told him, "Job, just curse God and die" (see Job 2:9). But Job knew that God is a God of restoration.

I've discovered two kinds of faith—a *delivering* faith and a *sustaining* faith. Delivering faith is when God instantly turns your situation around. When that happens, it's great. But it takes a greater faith and a deeper walk with God to have sustaining faith. Sustaining faith is what gets you through those dark nights of the soul when, like Job, you don't know where to go or what to do . . . but because of your faith in God, you do. Faith tells us the best is yet to come.

Better Days *Ahead*

Instead of their shame my people will receive a double portion, and instead of disgrace they will rejoice in their inheritance; and so they will inherit a double portion in their land, and everlasting joy will be theirs.

ISAIAH 61:7

*H*AVE YOU EXPERIENCED some unfair situations in which somebody did you wrong or mistreated you? Perhaps you are having problems in a relationship, or in your marriage, or with a child. Or maybe you've struggled financially, and you don't see how you can ever get ahead. Life has been one setback after another. If that sounds like you, I have good news for you: God wants to restore everything that has been stolen from you. He wants to restore your joy, peace, health, finances, and your family. And when God restores, He doesn't leave you as you were before bad things happened to you; He brings you out better than you were previously.

I have seen his ways, but I will heal him; I will guide him and restore comfort to him.

ISAIAH 57:18

With *Abundance*

GOD DOES NOT WANT to bring you out of your adversities all beaten up and bedraggled; no, you are not simply a survivor, you are "more than a conqueror" (see Romans 8:37). He wants to bring you out promoted and increased, with abundance. Beyond that, God wants to make the enemy pay for the wrongs done to you, His child. God wants to bring you out to a flourishing finish.

If you're in a tough situation today, you need to develop a restoration mentality. Mentally encourage yourself that God is going to turn your situation around. Remind yourself that you don't just defeat the enemy; you gather up all the spoils. Your attitude should be, *Father, I thank You, for I know I'm going to come out stronger, healthier, and happier than I've ever been.*

God Is a *Giver*

I have shown you in every way, by laboring like this, that you must support the weak. And remember the words of the Lord Jesus, that He said, "It is more blessed to give than to receive."

ACTS 20:35 NKJV

MANY PEOPLE NOWADAYS are blatantly and unashamedly living for themselves. Society teaches us to look out for number one. "What's in it for me?" We readily acknowledge this as the "me" generation, and that same narcissism sometimes spills over into our relationship with God, our families, and one another. Ironically, this selfish attitude condemns us to living shallow, unrewarding lives. No matter how much we acquire for ourselves, we are never satisfied.

God is a giver, and if you want to experience a new level of God's joy, if you want Him to pour out His blessing and favor in your life, then you must learn to be a giver and not a taker.

For God so loved the world, that he gave his only begotten Son.

JOHN 3:16 KJV

Created to Give

ONE OF THE GREATEST CHALLENGES WE face in our quest to enjoy our best lives now is the temptation to live selfishly. Because we believe that God wants the best for us, and that He wants us to prosper, it is easy to slip into the subtle trap of selfishness. Not only will you avoid that pitfall, but you will have more joy than you dreamed possible when you live to give, which is another major step to living at your full potential.

We were not made to function as self-involved people, thinking only of ourselves. No, God created us to be givers. And you will never be truly fulfilled as a human being until you learn the simple secret of how to give your life away. Have an attitude that says, *Who can I bless today?*

Start Sowing Seeds

"Or when did we see You sick, or in prison, and come to You?" And the King will answer and say to them, "Assuredly, I say to you, inasmuch as you did it to one of the least of these My brethren, you did it to Me."

MATTHEW 25:39–40 NKJV

*Y*OU MAY NOT REALIZE IT, but it is extremely selfish to go around always dwelling on your problems, always thinking about what you want or need, and hardly noticing the many needs of others all around you. One of the best things you can do if you're having a problem is to help solve somebody else's problem. If you want your dreams to come to pass, help someone else fulfill his or her dreams. Start sowing some seeds so God can bring you a harvest.

Think about this today: God will not fill a closed fist with good things.

A generous man will prosper;
he who refreshes others will himself
be refreshed.

PROVERBS 11:25

No "Lone Rangers"

WE WERE CREATED TO GIVE, not to simply please ourselves. If you miss that truth, you will miss the abundant, overflowing, joy-filled life that God has in store for you. But when you reach out to other people in need, God will make sure that your own needs are supplied. If you're down and discouraged, get your mind off yourself and go help meet someone else's need.

Perhaps you feel you have nothing to give. Sure you do! You can give a smile or a hug. You can do some menial but meaningful task to help someone. You can visit someone in the hospital or make a meal for a person who is shut in. You can write an encouraging letter. Somebody needs your friendship. God created us to be free, but He didn't make us to function as "Lone Rangers." We need one another.

Live to *Give*

Those who shut their ears to the cries of the poor will be ignored in their own time of need.

PROVERBS 21:13 NLT

OO MANY PEOPLE FOCUS ONLY on what they want, what they need, and what they feel will most benefit themselves, and they never get it. Quit trying to figure out what everybody can do for you, get your mind off yourself, start trying to figure out what you can do for somebody else, and go do it. Go visit the nursing home or a children's hospital. Call a friend and encourage that person. If you're struggling financially, go out and help somebody who has less than you have. For example, you could mow somebody's lawn or help them with something that needs to be fixed in their house. Somebody needs what you have to share. Somebody needs your love and encouragement.

If you want God to bless your life, live to give.

*But encourage one another daily,
as long as it is called Today, so that
none of you may be hardened
by sin's deceitfulness.*

HEBREWS 3:13

Encourage Others

WHEN YOU CENTER YOUR LIFE around yourself, not only do you miss out on God's best, but you rob other people of the joy and blessings that God wants to give them through you. It's easy to criticize and condemn, to point out everyone's flaws and failures. But God wants us to build people up, to be a blessing, speaking words of faith and victory into their lives.

It doesn't cost anything or take a lot of time to give somebody a compliment. What does it cost to tell your wife, "I love you. You're great. I'm glad you're mine"? How long does it take to tell your employee, "You are doing a fine job. I appreciate your hard work"? Do it today!

Always Blessed

Is it not to share your food with the hungry and to provide the poor wanderer with shelter— when you see the naked, to clothe him, and not to turn away from your own flesh and blood? Then your light will break forth like the dawn, and your healing will quickly appear; then your righteousness will go before you, and the glory of the LORD will be your rear guard.

ISAIAH 58:7–8

IT'S NOT ENOUGH TO simply think nice thoughts about others; we need to express them. As the old saying puts it: "Love is not love until you give it away." We should get up each morning with an attitude that says: *I'm going to make somebody else happy and meet their need today.* Something supernatural happens when we get our eyes off ourselves and turn to the needs of those around us. When you reach out to hurting people, God makes sure you are always blessed in abundance.

Sow for yourselves righteousness,
reap the fruit of unfailing love.

HOSEA 10:12

Reap the Fruit

WHEN MY MOTHER WAS diagnosed with terminal cancer, she could easily have come home and just sunk into a deep pit of depression. But she didn't stay focused on herself, and she refused to dwell on that sickness. In her time of greatest need, she went to church and prayed for other people who were sick and in need. She sowed those seeds of healing. And just as the Scripture says, as she began to help other people in need, her own healing came.

I'm convinced that many people would receive the miracle they are always praying about if they would simply turn their attention away from their own needs and problems and start to focus on being a blessing to other people. We need to look for opportunities to share God's love, His gifts, and His goodness with others.

Filled to Overflowing

Honor the LORD with your wealth, with the firstfruits of all your crops; then your barns will be filled to overflowing, and your vats will brim over with new wine.

PROVERBS 3:9–10

*I*F YOU WANT TO LIVE YOUR BEST LIFE now, you must develop a lifestyle of living to give instead of living to get. You can do this in many practical ways. If you have things lying around your house or in storage that you are never going to use again, why not give those things away to someone who could use them?

Our minds can conjure up all kinds of excuses when God begins unclasping our sticky fingers. Human nature wants to hold on to everything. But you probably have all sorts of other things that you haven't used in ages! If it's not meeting a need, turn it into a seed. Remember, we will reap what we sow.

Blessed to *Bless*

And I will make of you a great nation, and I will bless you [with abundant increase of favors] and make your name famous and distinguished, and you will be a blessing [dispensing good to others].

GENESIS 12:2 AMP

WE READ GOD'S PROMISE TO Abraham, and we often say, "All right, God! Come on; pour out Your blessings on me!" But notice, there's a catch. We must do something; better yet, we must be something. God is implying that we will not be blessed simply so we can live lavishly or self-indulgently. We will be blessed to be a blessing. Indeed, unless we are willing to be a blessing, God will not pour out His favor and goodness in our lives. We will receive from God in the same measure we give to others.

If we'd listen more carefully, maybe we'd hear God saying, "When are you going to start being a blessing?"

Start Where *You* Are

He who is kind to the poor lends to the LORD, and he will reward him for what he has done.

PROVERBS 19:17

*Y*OU MAY BE THINKING, *Well, if I had more money, I would give.* No, you have to start right where you are. You must be faithful with what you have, then God will trust you with more. You may not have much money, but you can buy somebody's dinner every once in a while. You can give somebody a kind word. You can go out of your way to pray for somebody in need.

Giving is a spiritual principle. Whatever you give will be given back to you. If you give a smile, you will receive smiles from others. If you are generous to people in their time of need, God will make sure that other people are generous to you in your time of need. What you make happen for others, God will make happen for you.

Give, and it will be given to you.
A good measure, pressed down,
shaken together and running over, will
be poured into your lap. For with
the measure you use, it will
be measured to you.

LUKE 6:38

Helping the Hurting

FRIEND, the closest thing to the heart of our God is helping hurting people. God loves when we sing and worship and pray. But nothing pleases God more than when we care for His children.

John Bunyan said, "You have not lived today until you have done something for someone who cannot pay you back." Be on the lookout for somebody you can bless. Somebody needs what you have to give. It may not be your money; it may be your time, your listening ear, your arms to encourage, or your smile to uplift. Who knows? Maybe just putting your arm around somebody and letting him or her know that you care can help begin to heal that person's heart.

Show *Kindness*

See that none of you repays another with evil for evil, but always aim to show kindness and seek to do good to one another and to everybody.

1 THESSALONIANS 5:15 AMP

*H*OW YOU TREAT OTHER people can have a great impact on the degree of blessings and favor of God you will experience in your life. Are you good to people? Are you kind and considerate? Do you speak and act with love in your heart and regard other people as valuable and special? Friend, you can't treat people poorly and expect to be blessed.

The Bible says we are to "aim to show kindness and seek to do good." We must be proactive. We should be on the lookout to share His mercy, kindness, and goodness with people. Moreover, we need to be kind and do good to people even when somebody is unkind to us. Evil is never overcome by more evil.

Love your enemies, do good to those who hate you, bless those who curse you, and pray for those who spitefully use you.

LUKE 6:27–28 NKJV

Walk in Love

*W*HEN SOMEBODY DOESN'T TREAT you right, you have a golden opportunity to help heal a wounded heart. Keep in mind, hurting people often hurt other people as a result of their own pain. If somebody is rude or inconsiderate, you can almost be certain that they have some unresolved issues inside. The last thing they need is for you to respond angrily.

Keep taking the high road and be kind and courteous. Walk in love and have a good attitude. God sees what you're doing, and He is your vindicator. He will make sure your good actions and attitude will overcome that evil. If you'll keep doing the right thing, you will come out far ahead of where you would have been had you fought fire with fire.

Aim for *Kindness*

If someone forces you to go one mile, go with him two miles.

MATTHEW 5:41

WHEN THAT COWORKER walks by you and doesn't give you the time of day, God expects you to go the extra mile and be friendly to him anyway. When that employee at the grocery store checkout counter is curt with you, your initial response may be to act rudely in return. That's the easy way; anybody can do that. Why not show them some of God's grace and mercy?

Aim for kindness and give them a word of encouragement. After all, you don't know what they may be going through. They may be living in hell on earth. If you return their venom with more vitriol, you could escalate the conflict, or your response could be the final straw that causes them to give up and sink into utter despair. Neither scenario is pleasing to God.

Love does no harm to its neighbor.
Therefore love is the fulfillment
of the law.

ROMANS 13:10

Kindness
Pays Off

*I*F YOU MISTREAT PEOPLE who are mistreating you, you will make matters worse. When you express anger to somebody who has been angry with you, it's like adding fuel to a fire. No, we overcome evil with good. When somebody hurts you, the only way you can overcome it is by showing them mercy, forgiving them, and doing what is right.

The Bible teaches us that God is our vindicator. He will not let you lose out. You may think you're getting the short end of the stick, but when it's all said and done, God will make sure that you don't lose anything truly valuable. Moreover, He'll make sure you get your just reward. Your responsibility is to remain calm and peaceable even when those around you are not.

Extend Mercy

As for you, you meant evil against me, but God meant it for good in order to bring about this present result, to preserve many people alive.

GENESIS 50:20 NASB

*I*F ANYBODY HAD A RIGHT TO return evil instead of love, it was Joseph. His brothers hated him so much, they purposed to kill him but then sold him into slavery. Years went by, and Joseph experienced all sorts of troubles and heartaches. But Joseph kept a good attitude, and God continued to bless him. After thirteen years of being in prison for a crime he didn't commit, God supernaturally promoted him to the second highest position in Egypt.

Can you imagine Joseph's brothers' fears when they came to Egypt and suddenly found their lives were in Joseph's hands? This was Joseph's opportunity to pay them back. Yet Joseph extended his mercy. Is it any wonder he was so blessed with God's favor? Joseph knew how to treat people right.

Love (God's love in us) does not insist on its own rights or its own way, for it is not self-seeking; it is not touchy or fretful or resentful; it takes no account of the evil done to it [it pays no attention to a suffered wrong].

1 CORINTHIANS 13:5 AMP

Love Overcomes Evil

YOU MAY HAVE PEOPLE IN your life who have done you great wrong, and you have a right to be angry and bitter. But if you will choose to let go of your grudge and forgive them, you can overcome that evil with good. You can get to the point where you can look at the people who have hurt you and return good for evil. If you do that, God will pour out His favor in your life in a fresh way. He will honor you, He will reward you, and He'll make those wrongs right.

God wants His people to help heal wounded hearts.

Show God's Goodness

Or do you despise the riches of His goodness, forbearance, and longsuffering, not knowing that the goodness of God leads you to repentance?

ROMANS 2:4 NKJV

*I*F SOMEBODY IS NOT TREATING YOU right, go out of your way to be kinder than usual to that person. If your husband is not serving God, don't go around beating him over the head with your Bible, preaching at him, nagging him, coercing him to attend church with you. No, just start being extra kind to him. Start loving him in a fresh way. God's goodness expressed through you will overcome evil. Friend, love never fails.

When you can bless your enemies and do good to those who have used or abused you, that's when God will take that evil and turn it around for good. Remember that God is in control. And when you bless your enemies, you will never lose. God will always make it up to you.

Abraham never wavered in believing God's promise. In fact, his faith grew stronger, and in this he brought glory to God.

ROMANS 4:20 NLT

When You *Believe*

IN OBEDIENCE TO GOD, Abraham moved all his flocks, his herds, his family, and even his extended family members to a new land. After living there for a while, they discovered that the portion of land where they settled wasn't able to support them with enough food and water for all the people and their flocks and herds. So Abraham offered his nephew Lot whichever part of the land he wanted (see Genesis 13). Taking advantage of his uncle's kindness, Lot took the beautiful valley with lush green pastures and rolling hills and ponds.

Abraham said, "Fine; go and be blessed." He could have said, "Lot, God spoke to me, not to you. I should get the first choice." Abraham didn't do that. He believed that God would make it up to him, and God did.

Lift *Your* Eyes

And the LORD said to Abram, after Lot had separated from him: "Lift your eyes now and look from the place where you are—northward, southward, eastward, and westward; for all the land which you see I give to you and your descendants forever."

GENESIS 13:14–15 NKJV

AFTER LOT TOOK THE BEST LAND and left Abraham with arid and barren land, Abraham must have been disappointed with his scruffy portion of the land. I'm sure he thought, *God, why do people always take advantage of my goodness? Lot wouldn't have had anything if I hadn't given it to him.*

However, God saw Abraham's integrity and said, "Because you treated your relative kindly, I'm going to give you an abundant blessing—hundreds and hundreds of acres; miles and miles of land. All that you can see is going to be yours." That's what He did for Abraham, and He can do it for you.

God is not unjust; he will not forget your work and the love you have shown him as you have helped his people and continue to help them.

HEBREWS 6:10

God Will *Not* Forget

MAYBE YOU FEEL THAT YOU'RE the one who's doing all the giving in some situation. Perhaps you are the parent of an ungrateful child. Maybe your former spouse is taking advantage of you in a divorce settlement. Possibly your company is talking about "downsizing" after you have given them the best years of your life. Because people know you are kind, generous, and friendly, they tend to take advantage of you or not appreciate you.

But God sees your heart. Nothing you do goes unnoticed by God. He's keeping the records, and He will reward you in due time. When you bless someone else, you never lose out. Even if someone takes advantage of your good nature, God will not allow your generosity to go unrewarded.

Do *Not* Grow Weary

But as for you, brethren, do not grow weary in doing good.

2 THESSALONIANS 3:13 NKJV

SOMETIMES WHEN WE'RE GOOD to people and we go the extra mile, we have a tendency to think, *I'm letting people walk all over me. I'm letting them take advantage of me. They're taking what rightfully belongs to me.*

That's when you have to say, "Nobody is taking anything from me. I am freely giving it to them. I'm blessing them on purpose, knowing that God is going to make it up to me." God is a just God, and He sees not just what you are doing but why you are doing it. God judges our motives as well as our actions. And because of your unselfishness, because you prefer others, because you're aiming for kindness, one day God will bless you for your gesture.

Live in harmony with one another; be sympathetic, love as brothers, be compassionate and humble.

1 PETER 3:8

Keep an *Open* Heart

EVERYWHERE YOU GO these days people are hurting and discouraged; many have broken dreams. They've made mistakes; their lives are in a mess. They need to feel God's compassion and His unconditional love. They don't need somebody to judge and criticize them. They need somebody to bring hope, to bring healing, to show God's mercy. Really, they are looking for a friend, somebody who will be there to encourage them, who will take the time to listen to their story and genuinely care.

If you want to live your best life now, you must make sure that you keep your heart of compassion open. We need to be on the lookout for people we can bless. We need to be willing to be interrupted and inconvenienced if it means we can help meet somebody else's need.

Be *Com-passionate*

If anyone has this world's goods (resources for sustaining life) and sees his brother and fellow believer in need, yet closes his heart of compassion against him, how can the love of God live and remain in him?

1 JOHN 3:17 AMP

OUR WORLD IS DESPERATE TO experience the love and compassion of our God. It is crying out for people with compassion, people who love unconditionally, people who will take some time to help their fellow sojourners on this planet. Certainly, when God created us, He put His supernatural love in all of our hearts. He's placed in you the potential to have a kind, caring, gentle, loving spirit. Because you are created in God's image, you have the moral capacity to experience God's compassion in your heart.

You have the opportunity to make a difference in other people's lives. You must learn to follow that love. Don't ignore it. Act on it. Somebody needs what you have.

The *Compassion* of Jesus

When [Jesus] saw the crowds, he had compassion on them, because they were harassed and helpless, like sheep without a shepherd. Then he said to his disciples, "The harvest is plentiful but the workers are few. Ask the Lord of the harvest, therefore, to send out workers into his harvest field."

MATTHEW 9:36–38

IF YOU STUDY THE LIFE OF JESUS, you will discover that He always took time for people. He was never too busy with His own agenda, with His own plans. He wasn't so caught up in Himself that He was unwilling to stop and help a person in need. He could have easily said, "Listen, I'm busy. I have a schedule to keep." But no, Jesus had compassion on people. He was concerned about what they were going through, and He willingly took time to meet their needs. He freely gave of His life. I believe He demands nothing less from those who claim to be His followers today.

Be a *Friend*

Filled with compassion, Jesus reached out his hand and touched the man. "I am willing," he said. "Be clean!" Immediately the leprosy left him and he was cured.

MARK 1:41–42

IF YOU WANT TO EXPERIENCE GOD'S abundant life, you must start taking time to help other people. Sometimes if we would just take the time to listen to people, we could help initiate a healing process in their lives. So many people have pain bottled up inside them. They have nobody they can talk to; they don't trust anybody. If you can open your heart of compassion and be that person's friend—without judging or condemning—and simply have an ear to listen, you may help lift that heavy burden.

You will be amazed at what a positive impact you can have if you will just learn to be a good listener. Learn to follow the flow of God's divine love.

This is love, that we walk according to His commandments. This is the commandment, that as you have heard from the beginning, you should walk in it.

2 JOHN 6 NKJV

Continual *Love*

WE'RE ALL SO BUSY. We have our own priorities and important plans and agendas. Often, our attitude is: *I don't want to be inconvenienced. Don't bother me with your problems. I've got enough problems of my own.* Too often, because of our own selfishness, we choose to close our hearts to others.

How can you tell if your heart is open or closed? Easy. Are you frequently concerned about other people, or are you concerned about only yourself? Do you take time to make a difference, to encourage others, to lift their spirits, to make people feel better about themselves? Do you follow the flow of love that God puts in your heart toward somebody in need… continually?

Be a *Good* Listener

My dear brothers, take note of this: Everyone should be quick to listen, slow to speak and slow to become angry.

JAMES 1:19

PEOPLE WHO HAVE CLOSED their hearts to compassion become self-involved and self-centered. Motivated by only what they want and what they think they need, they rarely are good listeners and seldom do anything for anybody else.

We need to learn to be good listeners. Don't always be so quick to give your opinion. Be sensitive to what the real need is in the person you hope to help. Too frequently, what we really want to do is just give them a quick word of encouragement, a semi-appropriate Scripture verse, and a fifteen-second prayer; then we can go on and do what we want to do. Instead, take the time today to hear someone with your heart, to show that person you are concerned and that you really care.

One man gives freely, yet gains even more; another withholds unduly, but comes to poverty.

PROVERBS 11:24

Change *Your* Focus

THE REASON MANY PEOPLE ARE NOT growing is because they are not sowing. They are living self-centered lives. Unless they change their focus and start reaching out to others, they will probably remain in a depressed condition, emotionally, financially, socially, and spiritually.

All through the Bible, we find the principle of sowing and reaping. "Whatever a man sows, that he will also reap" (Galatians 6:7 NKJV). Just as a farmer must plant some seeds if he hopes to reap a harvest, we, too, must plant some good seeds in the fields of our families, careers, businesses, and personal relationships. If you want to reap happiness, you have to sow some "happiness" seeds by making others happy. If you want to reap financial blessing, you must sow financial seeds in the lives of others. The seed always has to lead.

God Loves a *Cheerful* Giver

Whoever sows sparingly will also reap sparingly, and whoever sows generously will also reap generously. Each man should give what he has decided in his heart to give, not reluctantly or under compulsion, for God loves a cheerful giver.

2 CORINTHIANS 9:6–7

IN THE MIDST OF A GREAT FAMINE in the land of Canaan, Isaac did something that people without insight may have thought rather odd. He sowed seed and then reaped a hundredfold crop, because the Lord blessed him (see Genesis 26:12). In his time of need, Isaac didn't wait around, expecting someone else to come to his rescue. No, he acted in faith, and God supernaturally multiplied that seed.

Maybe you're in some sort of famine today. It could be a financial famine; or maybe you're simply famished for friends. Whatever the need, sow some seeds and reap a huge harvest.

Trust in the LORD and do good.
Then you will live safely in the land
and prosper.

PSALM 37:3 NLT

Do Something *Good*

IT'S NOT ENOUGH TO SAY, "God, I trust You. I know You are going to meet all my needs." That's like the farmer not planting any seeds and expecting a fabulous harvest. Scripture says there are two things we must do in times of trouble. First, we must trust in the Lord; and second, we must go out and do something good. Go out and sow some seeds. If you need a financial miracle, go buy somebody a cup of coffee this morning or give a little extra in the offering at church. If you don't have any money, do some physical work for somebody—mow somebody's lawn, pull some weeds, wash their windows. Make someone a pie. Do something to get some seed in the ground.

If you never plant the seeds, you'll wait forever for a harvest.

No More *Sitting* Around

For He satisfies the longing soul, and fills the hungry soul with goodness.

PSALM 107:9 NKJV

SOME PEOPLE SAY, "Joel, I've got a lot of problems of my own. I don't care about sowing seeds. I want to know how I can get out of my mess." This is how you can get out of your mess. If you want God to solve your problems, help solve somebody else's problem.

For instance, if you are lacking in friends, don't sit at home alone month after month, feeling sorry for yourself. Go to the nursing home or the hospital and find somebody you can cheer up. If you'll start sowing seeds of friendship, God will bring somebody great into your life. When you make other people happy, God will make sure that your life is filled with joy. Be more seed-oriented than need-oriented. Think about what kind of seed you can sow to get yourself out of that need.

All the believers were together and had everything in common. Selling their possessions and goods, they gave to anyone as he had need.

ACTS 2:44–45

In a *Time* of Need

I REMEMBER WHEN MY FATHER launched our church's first building program. We didn't have much money, but there was a little Spanish church down the street that had plans to construct a new sanctuary too. One Sunday morning my dad announced that we were going to take up a special offering, not for our new building, but for the Spanish church. Several thousand dollars came in that morning, which went straight down the road. The truth is, we needed the money more than they did, but Daddy understood the importance of getting some seed in the ground. Amazingly, it wasn't long before we had all the money we needed to get to work on our building project. We've lived by that principle ever since, and God has always met our needs.

Giving Gets God's Attention

And God is able to make all grace abound to you, so that in all things at all times, having all that you need, you will abound in every good work.

2 CORINTHIANS 9:8

IN THE BIBLE, a Roman named Cornelius and his family became the first recorded Gentile household to experience salvation after the resurrection of Jesus. Why was Cornelius chosen for this honor? Cornelius was told in a vision: "Your prayers and charities have not gone unnoticed by God!" (Acts 10:4 TLB). Friend, don't let anybody convince you that it doesn't make any difference whether you give. I'm not suggesting that you can buy miracles or that you have to pay God to meet your needs. But I am saying that God sees your gifts and acts of kindness. It pleases God when you give, and He will pour out His favor on you.

> *Give generously, for your gifts will return to you later. Divide your gifts among many, for in the days ahead you yourself may need much help.*
>
> ECCLESIASTES 11:1–2 TLB

Generosity Is Repaid

GOD IS KEEPING A RECORD of every good deed you've ever done. You may think it went unnoticed, but God saw it. And in your time of need, He will make sure that somebody is there to help you. Your generous gifts will come back to you. God has seen every smile you've ever given to a hurting person. He's observed every time you went out of the way to lend a helping hand. God has witnessed when you have given sacrificially. God has promised that your generous gifts will come back to you (see Luke 6:38). In your time of need, because of your generosity, God will move heaven and earth to make sure you are taken care of.

Supplying *Others'* Needs

This service that you perform is not only supplying the needs of God's people but is also overflowing in many expressions of thanks to God.

2 CORINTHIANS 9:12

SOME FIRST-CENTURY CHRISTIANS were struggling to survive in the Greek region of Macedonia. The Bible says that they were in deep poverty and deep trouble (see 2 Corinthians 8:2). What did they do in their time of need? Did they say, "God, why do we have so much trouble coming against us?" Not at all. The Scripture records that in the midst of their great trouble, they stayed full of joy and they gave generously to others. They knew if they would help to meet other people's needs, God would meet theirs.

In your times of difficulty, do just what they did. Number one, stay full of joy. Number two, go out and sow a seed. Help someone else, and you will be helped.

> For the eyes of the LORD range
> throughout the earth to strengthen
> those whose hearts are fully committed
> to him.
>
> 2 CHRONICLES 16:9

Sow a *Special* Seed

PERHAPS YOU ARE HOPING TO buy a new home or to get out of debt. Sow a special seed that relates to your specific need. We can't buy God's goodness, but we can exercise our faith through our giving.

Early in our marriage, Victoria and I decided to sell our townhome and buy a house. For eight months, we never received a serious offer. At the time, we were making double mortgage payments on the townhome to pay the principal down sooner. We decided to sow the second part of that money as a seed, giving it to God's work. We did that faithfully for several months, trusting for God's favor. God not only brought us a buyer, but we sold our townhouse for even more than we were hoping for!

Prepare the Way

Delight yourself in the LORD and he will give you the desires of your heart.

PSALM 37:4

SOME PEOPLE WILL TELL YOU THAT IT doesn't make any difference whether you give or not, or that it doesn't do any good. But don't listen to those lies. God is keeping those records.

Friend, if you want to live your best life now, don't hoard what God has given you. Learn to sow it in faith. Put some action behind your prayers. Do something out of the ordinary as an expression of your faith. If you are believing for a promotion at work, don't just say, "God, I'm counting on You." Certainly, you should pray, but do more than pray. Go out and feed the poor, or do something to get some seed in the ground that God can bless. Remember, when you give, you are preparing the way for God to meet your needs today and in the future.

This is the day which the LORD has made; let us rejoice and be glad in it.

PSALM 118:24 NASB

Happiness Is Your Choice

*I*T IS A SIMPLE YET PROFOUND TRUTH: happiness is a choice. You don't have to wait for everything to be perfect in your family or with your business. You don't have to forgo happiness until you lose weight, break an unhealthy habit, or accomplish all your goals. Happiness is your choice.

You might as well choose to be happy and enjoy your life! When you do that, not only will you feel better, but your faith will cause God to show up and work wonders. To do so, you must learn to live in today, one day at a time; better yet, make the most of this moment. It's good to set goals and make plans, but if you're always living in the future, you're never really enjoying the present in the way God wants us to.

Grace for Today

Peace I leave with you; My peace I give to you; not as the world gives do I give to you. Do not let your heart be troubled, nor let it be fearful.

JOHN 14:27 NASB

WE NEED TO UNDERSTAND that God gives us the grace to live today. He has not yet given us tomorrow's grace, and we should not worry about it. Learn to live one day at a time. By an act of your will, choose to start enjoying your life right now. Learn to enjoy your family, friends, health, and work; enjoy everything in your life. Happiness is a decision you make, not an emotion you feel. God gives us His peace on the inside, but it's up to us to tap into God's supernatural peace.

To enjoy your best life now is to choose to be happy this morning. Life is too short not to enjoy every single day.

> *Let the peace of Christ rule in your hearts, since as members of one body you were called to peace. And be thankful.*
>
> COLOSSIANS 3:15

Let *Peace* Rule

WE ALL HAVE DIFFICULTIES, struggles, and challenges, but if we make the mistake of allowing those circumstances to dictate our happiness, we risk missing out on God's abundant life. It was never His intention for us to live one day "on cloud nine," and the next day down in the dumps because we have problems. God wants us to live consistently and enjoy every single day of our lives.

Another negative comes when we focus so much on the future that we get anxious because we don't know what's coming. Naturally, the uncertainty increases our stress level and creates a sense of insecurity. When we get to tomorrow, God will give us what we need. But if we're worried about tomorrow right now, we are bound to be frustrated and discouraged.

You *Can* Do It

No temptation has seized you except what is common to man. And God is faithful; he will not let you be tempted beyond what you can bear. But when you are tempted, he will also provide a way out so that you can stand up under it.

1 CORINTHIANS 10:13

CERTAINLY THERE ARE TIMES in all our lives when bad things happen, or things don't turn out as we had hoped. We can choose to be unhappy and go around with a sour attitude or to be happy in spite of our circumstances.

"Joel, I can't do that," you may say. "I get upset easily." No—you can do whatever you want to do. God said He would never let us go through something that is too difficult for us to handle. And if your desire is great enough, you can stay calm and cool no matter what comes against you in life.

Cast all your anxiety on him because he cares for you.

1 PETER 5:7

Keep *Your* Peace

I ONCE HAD AN OLDER MODEL WHITE Lexus that hardly had a scratch. One day, Victoria took it to the car wash with those supersoft brushes that barely touch the car. Unfortunately, something was out of alignment, and it put an awful scratch from the front bumper all the way up the hood and over the roof to the back windshield! When I saw the damage, I immediately had a decision to make. I could get angry and allow this accident to steal my joy, or I could keep my peace, knowing that God was in control. I decided to look at the bright side. I said to Victoria, "Well, I'm the only guy in Houston who's got a Lexus with a racing stripe right down the center."

Even in the pressure points of life, we can choose to tap into God's peace.

This *Is* the Day

Now listen, you who say, "Today or tomorrow we will go to this or that city, spend a year there, carry on business and make money." Why, you do not even know what will happen tomorrow. What is your life? You are a mist that appears for a little while and then vanishes.

JAMES 4:13–14

When negative things happen to us, no matter how much we yell and scream, murmur and complain, it's not going to make anything better. We might as well keep our peace and stay happy.

Life is flying by, so don't waste another moment of your precious time being angry, unhappy, or worried. David tells us "this is the day" in which we should rejoice and be glad (Psalm 118:24). He didn't say, "Tomorrow or next week." No, he said, "This is the day." This is the day that God wants you to choose to be happy.

Trust in the LORD with all thine heart; and lean not unto thine own understanding. In all thy ways acknowledge him, and he shall direct thy paths.

PROVERBS 3:5–6 KJV

God Is in Control

THINGS MAY NOT BE PERFECT in your life, but if you hope to get to where you want to go, you must be happy right where you are. Many people assume that they are not going to be happy until their circumstances change—until their spouse changes, or until they get a bigger house, or until they get rid of all their problems.

Don't make that mistake. Enjoy your life right where you are. Maybe you have some major obstacles in your path, but being discouraged is not going to make anything better. You need to realize that God is in control of your life. He's directing your steps, and He has you exactly where He wants you.

God Has a *Purpose*

But godliness with contentment is great gain.

1 TIMOTHY 6:6

THE APOSTLE PAUL SAID, "I have learned how to be content (satisfied to the point where I am not disturbed or disquieted) in whatever state I am" (Philippians 4:11 AMP). He was saying, "I've made a decision that I'm going to live my life happy." Now "content" doesn't mean we don't want to see change or we simply sit back in neutral and accept everything as it comes.

That's the key. You don't have to get upset because your circumstances are not exactly what you want them to be. Keep in mind that God will not allow a difficulty to come into your life, unless He has a purpose for it. If you'll keep the right attitude, God has promised He will turn that situation around in your favor, and you will come out better off than you were before.

There is a time for everything, and a season for every activity under heaven: a time to be born and a time to die, a time to plant and a time to uproot.

ECCLESIASTES 3:1–2

Through the Dry Season

WE ALL GO THROUGH dry seasons in our lives, times when we don't see anything happening. Maybe you've been praying and believing, but your prayers aren't being answered; or, you're giving, but you don't seem to be getting anything in return. Maybe you are doing your best to treat people right; you're going the extra mile to help others, but nobody is going out of their way to help you. What's going on? Is God's Word a lie? Do these principles not work?

No, these dry seasons are proving grounds. God wants to see how you are going to respond. What kind of attitude will you have when you are doing the right thing, but the wrong thing keeps happening to you?

Keep Doing What's *Right*

I wait for the LORD, my soul waits, and in his word I put my hope. My soul waits for the LORD more than watchmen wait for the morning.

PSALM 130:5–6

DURING THE LATE 1950s, my father was the successful pastor of a large congregation that had just built a brand-new sanctuary. But about that time, my sister Lisa was born with a birth injury, something similar to cerebral palsy. That was one of the darkest hours of my parents' lives. They searched the Scriptures, and their eyes were opened to the message of healing. However, the idea of a contemporary, miracle-working God was not received well by the church, and my heartbroken father eventually left that church and had to start all over with ninety other people in an abandoned feed store.

In that dark time, Daddy kept doing what he knew was right. God was preparing him for greater things.

My flesh and my heart may fail, but God is the Rock and firm Strength of my heart and my Portion forever.

PSALM 73:26 AMP

Times of *Preparation*

ON MOTHER'S DAY 1959, my father and mother opened Lakewood Church in a rundown building with holes in the floor. For nearly thirteen years that tiny congregation hardly grew at all. It was an extremely dry season in my father's life. He had gone from speaking to thousands of people to laboring in obscurity. But God was doing a work in my father, and those years were a time of testing. Daddy knew if he remained faithful in the tough times, God would promote him, which is exactly what happened. Millions of people have been touched through the ministry of Lakewood Church.

When you go through a long period of time when you don't see anything good happening, just stay faithful; keep a smile on your face, and keep doing what you know is right. God is preparing you for greater things.

Stay Full of Joy

A happy heart makes the face cheerful ...the cheerful heart has a continual feast.

PROVERBS 15:13, 15

THE APOSTLE PAUL WROTE MANY of his letters while incarcerated, often in prison cells not much bigger than a small bathroom. Some historians and Bible commentators believe that the raw sewage system of that day ran right through one of the dungeons in which he was imprisoned. Yet Paul wrote such amazing faith-filled words as, "I can do all things through Christ who strengthens me" (Philippians 4:13 NKJV). And "Rejoice in the Lord always. Again I will say, rejoice!" (Philippians 4:4 NKJV).

Notice that we are to rejoice and be happy at all times. In your difficulties, when things aren't going your way, make a decision to stay full of joy.

A cheerful heart is good medicine, but a crushed spirit dries up the bones.

PROVERBS 17:22

Joy Is Your Strength

YOU NEED TO UNDERSTAND that the enemy is not really after your dreams, your health, or your finances. He's not primarily after your family. He's after your joy. The Bible says that "the joy of the LORD is your strength" (Nehemiah 8:10 NKJV), and your enemy knows if he can deceive you into living down in the dumps and depressed, you are not going to have the necessary strength—physically, emotionally, or spiritually—to withstand his attacks.

When you rejoice in the midst of your difficulties, you're giving the enemy a black eye. He doesn't know what to do with people who keep giving God praise despite their circumstances. Learn how to smile and laugh. Quit being so uptight and stressed out. Make your choice to enjoy your life to the fullest today.

Trust God Anyway

The LORD directs our steps, so why try to understand everything along the way?

PROVERBS 20:24 NLT

*I*SN'T IT INTERESTING THAT WE BELIEVE God is guiding us as long as we are getting what we want and we're "living on the mountaintop," relatively unscathed by the warp and woof of life in the valley below? But we need to understand that the Lord is directing our steps even when it seems things are not going our way. You may be in a stressful situation this morning. You may be thinking, *This doesn't seem right. God, I don't understand it.*

Friend, you are never going to understand everything you go through in life or why certain things come against you. You simply must learn to trust God anyway. You must learn to keep a good attitude in the midst of the chaos and confusion, knowing that God is still in control.

A man's heart plans his way, but the
LORD directs his steps.

PROVERBS 16:9 NKJV

God's Way

*I*N THE LATE 1990s, two former college basketball players missed their connecting flight to Kenya. Nine irritating hours later, the only seats remaining in the next available flight were in first class, so the two big men were seated at the front of the plane. Midway through that flight, the plane took a nosedive and plummeted toward the ground at full throttle. At the sound of commotion, a flight attendant opened the cockpit door, and there was a huge deranged man who had overwhelmed the pilots. The two basketball players jumped up and wrestled the attacker to the ground and subdued him. Without their assistance, the plane would have crashed within seconds, having already fallen from thirty thousand feet to less than four thousand feet.

God delayed those two young men on purpose and put them strategically where they could help save that entire plane. If He redirects our steps, He has a reason.

God's Guidance Works

The LORD will continually guide you, and satisfy your desire in scorched places, and give strength to your bones; and you will be like a watered garden, and like a spring of water whose waters do not fail.

ISAIAH 58:11 NASB

SOMETIMES GOD WILL PUT you in an uncomfortable situation so you can help somebody else. You may be living with a spouse or a child who is difficult to get along with. Or perhaps you work in an office that is filled with favoritism or politics. God knows what He's doing. He can see the big picture; He can see the future. And He has you exactly where He wants you today.

Quit questioning Him and start trusting Him. Just know that God is in control. He has your best interests at heart. Trust Him today to direct your steps and to cause you to be right where you need to be at just the right time.

Whatever you do, do your work heartily, as for the Lord rather than for men, knowing that from the Lord you will receive the reward of the inheritance. It is the Lord Christ whom you serve.

COLOSSIANS 3:23–24 NASB

Be a Person of *Excellence*

*M*ANY PEOPLE WANT TO DO AS LITTLE as they possibly can and still get by. But God did not create us to be mediocre. He doesn't want us to just barely get by, or to do what everybody else is doing. God has called us to be people of excellence and integrity. Indeed, the only way to be truly happy is to live with excellence and integrity. Any hint of compromise will taint our greatest victories or our grandest achievements.

Remember: you represent Almighty God. How you live, how you conduct your business and do your work, is all a reflection on our God. If you want to live your best life now, start aiming for excellence in everything you do.

No Compromises

Do you see a man who excels in his work? He will stand before kings; he will not stand before unknown men.

PROVERBS 22:29 NKJV

A PERSON OF EXCELLENCE and integrity goes the extra mile to do what's right. He keeps his word even when it's difficult. People of excellence give their employers a full day's work; they don't come in late, leave early, or call in sick when they are not. When you have an excellent spirit, it shows up in the quality of your work, and the attitude with which you do it.

God's people are people of excellence. Subtle compromises of excellence will keep us from God's best. Whatever we do, we should give our best effort and do it as if we were doing it for God. If we'll work with that standard in mind, God promises to reward us, and others will be attracted to our God.

I put in charge of Jerusalem my brother Hanani, along with Hananiah the commander of the citadel, because he was a man of integrity and feared God more than most men do.

NEHEMIAH 7:2

If *You* Feel Stuck

LOT OF PEOPLE SHOW UP at work fifteen minutes late, then they wander around the office, go get some coffee, and finally get to their desk or workstation thirty minutes later. They spend half the day engaged in personal telephone calls, playing games, or sending jokes on the Internet, and then they wonder, *God, why don't You ever bless me? Why don't I ever get a promotion?*

There may be many factors, of course, but one thing is for sure: God doesn't bless mediocrity; He blesses excellence. If you're stuck in a rut while others are being blessed and continuing to prosper and get ahead, consider whether the problem is one of your own making. Are you a person of excellence and integrity?

Be *Your* Best

> *The man of integrity walks securely,*
> *but he who takes crooked paths will be*
> *found out.*
>
> PROVERBS 10:9

PEOPLE SAY TO ME, "But Joel, everybody's doing it. Everybody gets to work late at my office. Everybody surfs the Internet when the boss is gone. Everybody takes extra-long lunch breaks." Maybe so, but you are not like everybody else! You are called to live a life of excellence. Start making the more excellent choices in every area of life, even in mundane matters such as paying your bills on time. Do a little bit more than you are required to do. If you are supposed to be at work at eight o'clock, get there ten minutes early and stay ten minutes late. Go the extra mile. Don't go out looking unkempt, undisciplined, sloppy, and less than your best.

In everything you do, attempt to represent God well.

Do Things *Well*

"Well done, my good servant!" his master replied. "Because you have been trustworthy in a very small matter, take charge of ten cities."

LUKE 19:17

TAKE PRIDE IN WHAT GOD HAS GIVEN you. You may be driving an old car, but that's no excuse for not keeping it clean and neat. Similarly, you may have an old small home, but make sure it looks like a person of excellence lives there.

God's people are people of excellence. They stand out from the crowd because they choose to do things well. You may be in a situation today where everybody around you is compromising their integrity or taking the easy way out. Don't let that rub off on you. Be the one to have an excellent spirit. Do your work well, take care of the resources that God has given you, and live in such a manner that when people see you, they will be attracted to your God.

Be a Person of *Integrity*

Whoever can be trusted with very little can also be trusted with much, and whoever is dishonest with very little will also be dishonest with much.

LUKE 16:10

GOD WANTS US TO BE people of integrity, people of honor, people who are trustworthy. A person of integrity is open and honest and true to his word. He doesn't have any hidden agendas or ulterior motives. He doesn't need a legal contract to force him to fulfill his commitments. People of integrity are the same in private as they are in public. They do what's right whether anybody is watching or not.

God will only trust us with more after we have been faithful with a little. Remember, our lives are an open book before God. He looks at our hearts and motives. There's no limit to what God will do in your life when He knows that He can trust you.

Catch all the foxes, those little foxes,
before they ruin the vineyard of love,
for the grapevines are blossoming!

SONG OF SOLOMON 2:15 NLT

Do the *Right* Thing

IF YOU DON'T HAVE INTEGRITY, you will never reach your highest potential. Integrity is the foundation on which a truly successful life is built. Every time you compromise, every time you are less than honest, you are causing a slight crack in the foundation. If you continue compromising, that foundation will never be able to hold what God wants to build. You'll never have lasting prosperity if you don't first have integrity. You may enjoy some temporary success, but you'll never see the fullness of God's favor if you don't take the high road and make the more excellent choices. On the other hand, God's blessings will overtake us if we settle for nothing less than living with integrity.

Be willing to pay the price to do the right thing.

God Is Watching

O LORD, you have searched me and you know me. You know when I sit and when I rise; you perceive my thoughts from afar.

PSALM 139:1–2

HAVE YOU EVER FELT as though somebody was watching you? Guess what? People are watching you. They're watching how you dress, how you care for your home, how you treat other people. They are trying to determine whether your words and your walk—your lifestyle—are consistent. What do they see? Are you a good representation of our God? Are you striving for excellence? Or are you compromising in so-called insignificant areas?

Oh, and your heavenly Father is also watching. What is He seeing? Are you true to your word, or do you have hidden agendas or ulterior motives? Do you treat your friends kindly and then go home and treat your family rudely? Live this day to please Him, and you will be pleased with yourself.

*Don't lie to each other, for you have
stripped off your old sinful nature and
all its wicked deeds.*

COLOSSIANS 3:9

Speak the *Truth*

EVERY DAY OUR INTEGRITY IS TESTED.
If a cashier gives you too much money in return,
are you going to have integrity and make things
right? Do you call in sick at work so you can stay
home and take care of personal business, go to the
beach, or go play golf? When the boss asks how
things are going, do you inflate the figures in your
favor? When the phone rings and it's somebody
you don't want to talk to, do you tell your child to
say, "Tell them I'm not home"?

"Little white lies" are lies. In God's sight, there
is no such thing as a white, gray, or black lie. If you're
not telling the truth, that's being dishonest. Sooner or
later, it will catch up to you. What you sow you will
eventually reap.

Be Honest

Buy the truth and do not sell it; get wisdom, discipline and understanding.

PROVERBS 23:23

WHY FUSS ABOUT "WHITE LIES"? If you will lie about the little things, before long you'll lie about bigger things. The people in large companies that have come tumbling down because of financial misdeeds didn't start off by stealing millions of dollars. They started off compromising a hundred dollars here, a thousand dollars there. Then, when the opportunity came, they compromised millions.

Don't kid yourself. If you will compromise in something small, eventually you will compromise in more serious matters. Compromise is a downhill slide. Theft is theft, whether it's one dollar or a thousand dollars. Taking home your company's office supplies is dishonesty. Not giving your company a full day's work is not integrity. Stretching the truth in order to get a new account is deceit. God won't bless any of that.

And my honesty will testify for me in the future, whenever you check on the wages you have paid me.

GENESIS 30:33

Integrity and Prosperity

W E NEED TO LIVE HONESTLY before our God and before other people. I heard somebody put it this way: "Don't do anything that you wouldn't feel comfortable reading about in the newspaper the next day." It's not always easy. Are we paying our debts? Are we being aboveboard in our business decisions? Are we treating other people with respect and honor?

Integrity and prosperity are flip sides of the same coin. You can't have one without the other. God may be reminding you about something such as paying a bill that you've swept under the rug. Maybe it's about getting to work on time consistently; maybe you know you should be more truthful with your wife. Start making things right. Step up to a higher level of integrity in those areas.

A *Clear* Conscience

I strive always to keep my conscience clear before God and man.

ACTS 24:16

YOU MAY NOT THINK it makes any difference when you don't pay your bills on time or if you treat your friends one way and your spouse another. But if you don't learn to pass those tests, God will not promote you. Remember, our lives are an open book before God. He looks at our hearts. He looks at our motives. God sees every time you go the extra mile to do what's right. He also sees the times that you compromise and take the easy way out.

Learn to listen to your conscience. God put that inside you so you would have an inner rule by which to know right from wrong. When you start to compromise, you will hear that alarm go off in your conscience. Don't ignore it. Do what you know in your heart is the right thing.

His word is in my heart like a fire,
a fire shut up in my bones. I am weary
of holding it in; indeed, I cannot.

JEREMIAH 20:9

Live
Inspired!

*L*ET'S NOT BE NAÏVE. The pressures, tensions, and stress of modern life constantly threaten to take a toll on our enthusiasm for living. You probably know some people who have lost their passion. They've lost their zest for life. Once they were excited about the future, but they've lost their fire. I especially see this happening when people get accustomed to God's goodness; living by grace becomes routine.

The word *enthusiasm* derives from two Greek words: *en theos*, meaning "inspired by God." Living your best life now is living with enthusiasm and being excited about the life God has given you. It is believing for more good things in the days ahead, but it is also living in the moment and enjoying it to the hilt! Start today.

Never Take God for Granted

And hope does not disappoint us, because God has poured out his love into our hearts by the Holy Spirit, whom he has given us.

ROMANS 5:5

ONE OF THE MAIN REASONS WE LOSE our enthusiasm in life is because we start to take for granted what God has done for us. Don't allow your relationship with Him to become stale or your appreciation for His goodness to become common. Don't take for granted the greatest gift of all that God has given you—Himself!

We need to stir ourselves up, to replenish our supply of God's good gifts on a daily basis. Like the Israeli people in the wilderness who had to gather God's miraculous provisions of manna afresh each morning, we, too, cannot get by on yesterday's supply. We need fresh enthusiasm each day. Our lives need to be inspired, infused, filled afresh with God's goodness every day. Stay filled with hope today.

Never lag in zeal and in earnest endeavor; be aglow and burning with the Spirit, serving the Lord.

ROMANS 12:11 AMP

Be the *Happiest*

GOD'S PEOPLE SHOULD BE the happiest people on earth! So happy, in fact, that other people notice. Why? Because we not only have a fabulous future, but we can enjoy life today! That's what living your best life now is all about.

Don't just go through the motions in life. Make a decision that you are not going to live another day without the joy of the Lord in your life; without love, peace, and passion; without being excited about your life. And understand that you don't have to have something extraordinary happening in your life to be excited. You may not have the perfect job or the perfect marriage or live in the perfect environment, but you can still choose to live each day aglow with God's presence.

Staying *Inspired*

Be filled with the Spirit. Speak to one another with psalms, hymns and spiritual songs. Sing and make music in your heart to the Lord.

EPHESIANS 5:18–19

*I*T'S NOT ALWAYS EASY TO stay excited and inspired. Perhaps at one time you were deeply in love, full of passion, but now your marriage has become stale and stagnant. Or maybe you were excited about your job, but it's become dull and boring. Maybe at one time you were excited about serving God. You couldn't wait to get to church. You loved reading your Bible, praying, and spending time with fellow believers. But lately you've been thinking, *I don't know what's wrong with me. I don't have any passion. I'm just going through the motions.*

The truth is, much of life is routine, and we can become stagnant if we're not careful to stay filled with the Holy Spirit. He alone can renew our spirit daily.

Be very careful, then, how you live—not as unwise but as wise, making the most of every opportunity, because the days are evil. Therefore do not be foolish, but understand what the Lord's will is.

EPHESIANS 5:15–17

Live *Wisely*

ARE YOU ON FIRE WITH ENTHUSIASM this morning? You can be! When you awaken in the morning, you can get up with passion to meet the day. You can remain excited about your dreams. You can go to work each day with enthusiasm.

"Well, I don't really like my job," someone complains. "I can't stand driving in the traffic. I don't like the people I work around." If that sounds familiar, you need to change your attitude. You should be grateful that you have a job. You need to appreciate and stay excited about the opportunities God has given you. Wherever you are in life, make the most of it and be the best that you can be.

Joy in Serving

Sitting down, Jesus called the Twelve and said, "If anyone wants to be first, he must be the very last, and the servant of all."

MARK 9:35

LIVING LIFE WITH ENTHUSIASM includes raising your children. Don't get up and say, "Humph! My friends are out doing something fun and exciting. All I'm doing is taking care of kids." A parent's work is one of the most important jobs in the whole world. But you may not have somebody patting you on the back or cheering you on. Your day may not be filled with extraordinary events. There are diapers to change, children to feed, housework that needs to be done; routine, mundane chores that start over the moment you complete them.

But in the midst of the ordinary, you can choose to have an extraordinary attitude toward your work. The Scripture tells us to do everything we do with our whole hearts, "to never lag in zeal" (Romans 12:11 AMP).

For you yourselves know how you ought to follow our example. . . . We worked night and day, laboring and toiling so that we would not be a burden to any of you.

2 THESSALONIANS 3:7–8

Set an *Example*

WHEN YOU GET TO WORK TODAY, don't give your employer a halfhearted effort. Don't dawdle on the telephone, wasting your employer's time and money. If you are digging a ditch, don't spend half the day leaning on your shovel; do your work with excellence and enthusiasm!

"Well," someone says, "they don't pay me enough, anyway. I shouldn't have to work very hard." Friend, you won't be blessed with that kind of attitude. God wants you to give it everything you've got. Be enthusiastic. Set an example. Do your work with such excellence that others will be impressed with your God merely by observing your positive work ethic. Be so full of joy that other people will want what you have.

Be Like *Christ*

I have given you an example to follow. Do as I have done to you. I tell you the truth, slaves are not greater than their master. Nor is the messenger more important than the one who sends the message. Now that you know these things, God will bless you for doing them.

JOHN 13:15–17 NLT

ASK YOURSELF, "Is the way I'm living attractive and contagious? Will my attitudes, the words I speak, my expressions, the way I handle challenges and setbacks, cause anybody to want what I have?" In other words, are you drawing people to God because of your joy, your friendliness, your enthusiasm, your attitude of faith? Or do you alienate people, turning them away because you're perpetually negative, discouraged, caustic, or cynical? Nobody enjoys being around a person like that. If you want to point people to God, or simply to a better way of living, have some enthusiasm and be excited about life.

Whatever your hand finds to do, do it with all your might.

ECCLESIASTES 9:10

Keep *It* Going

THERE'S A TRAFFIC POLICEMAN WHO worked by the Galleria, one of the busy shopping areas in Houston. During rush hour, the traffic was so bad you could wait ten or fifteen minutes just to get through one light. Drivers would get so upset, but when they approached the policeman, their whole attitude changed. He didn't simply direct traffic; he put on a show! He was practically dancing as he directed that traffic, with both arms waving wildly, his hands gesturing, his feet shuffling all through the intersection, all at the same time! Amazingly, after inching along in the traffic jam, many drivers would pull over into nearby parking lots just to watch.

Don't just show up for work and go through the motions. Passionately fulfill your destiny.

Give It Your All

You have filled my heart with greater joy than when their grain and new wine abound.

PSALM 4:7

*I*N THE NEW TESTAMENT, the apostle Paul encouraged his young coworker Timothy to "fan the flame and stir up the gift that is within you" (see 2 Timothy 1:6). Paul was reminding his understudy to live with enthusiasm. Give it your all. Don't settle for mediocrity. Stir yourself up; rekindle that fire.

You may have to live or work around people who are prone to being negative, who tend to drag you down. But don't let their lack of enthusiasm squelch your passion. If you live with a deadbeat spouse, make a decision that you're going to be happy and enthusiastic anyway. If your parents are always negative, try to overcome that negativity by being positive, encouraging, and uplifting. Fan your flame more than usual to make sure the fire doesn't go out.

...for everyone born of God overcomes the world. This is the victory that has overcome the world, even our faith.

1 JOHN 5:4

Stay on Fire

*D*O YOU WANT YOUR LIFE TO make an impact this morning? You can change the atmosphere of your home or your entire office with a little bit of enthusiasm. Choose to be happy; live with excellence and integrity, and put a spring in your step. Put a smile on your face, and let the world know that you are enjoying the life God has given you!

When everybody else is down and defeated, when you are all alone with nobody nearby to encourage you, simply encourage yourself. Your attitude should be: *It doesn't matter what anybody else does or doesn't do, I'm going to live my life with enthusiasm! I'm going to stay on fire. I'm going to be aglow. I'm going to be passionate about seeing my dreams come to pass.*

Fruit of the Spirit

But the fruit of the Spirit is love, joy, peace, patience, kindness, goodness, faithfulness, gentleness and self-control. Against such things there is no law.

GALATIANS 5:22–23

*P*EOPLE WHO SEE ME ON television sometimes write to me, saying, "Joel, why do you always smile so much? Why are you so happy?" "I'm glad you asked!" I respond, and that opens the door for me to tell them about my relationship with God, and how they can have a relationship with Him as well.

Some guy stopped me on the street in New York City and said, "Hey, aren't you that smiling preacher?" I laughed and said, "I guess so. That's me. I'm the smiling preacher." I take that as a compliment. Yes, I'm guilty of being happy! I'm guilty of being excited about the future. That's what it means to stay full of zeal. Stay on fire and aglow. Whatever you do, do it with enthusiasm!

If you are willing and obedient,
you will eat the best from the land.

ISAIAH 1:19

A *Satisfied* Life

*N*OTICE, IF WE OBEY GOD and are willing to trust Him, we will have the best this life has to offer—and more! But God says we have to be willing to obey.

Friend, God doesn't want you to drag through life defeated and depressed. No matter what you've been through, no matter whose fault it was, no matter how impossible your situation may look, the good news is that God wants to turn it around and restore everything that has been stolen from you. He wants to restore your marriage, your family, your career. He wants to restore those broken dreams. He wants to restore your joy and give you a peace and happiness you've never known before. Most of all, He wants to restore your relationship with Him. God wants you to live a satisfied life.

Total Victory

...and to know this love that surpasses knowledge—that you may be filled to the measure of all the fullness of God.

EPHESIANS 3:19

*G*OD IS IN THE LONG-TERM restoration business. He wants you to have a life filled with an abundance of joy and happiness. God doesn't want you simply to survive that marriage. God wants to turn it around and restore you with a strong, healthy, rewarding relationship. God doesn't want your business to merely make it through the murky economic waters. He wants your business to sail and to excel! When God restores, He has a vision of total victory for your life!

Hold on to that new enlarged vision of victory that God has given you. Start expecting things to change in your favor. Dare to boldly declare that you are standing strong against the forces of darkness. You will not settle for a life of mediocrity!

Stir up (rekindle the embers of, fan the flame of, and keep burning) the [gracious] gift of God, [the inner fire] that is in you.

2 TIMOTHY 1:6 AMP

Your *Best* Life Now

RIEND, IF YOU WANT TO SEE GOD'S favor, do everything with your whole heart. Do it with passion and some fire. Give it your all. Not only will you feel better, but that fire will spread, and soon other people will want what you have. Wherever you are in life, make the most of it and be the best you can be.

Raise your level of expectancy. Stay passionate about seeing your dreams come to pass. It's our faith that activates the power of God. Let's quit limiting Him with our small-minded thinking and start believing Him for bigger and better things. God will take you places you've never dreamed of, and you will be having your best life now.

NOTES

NOTES